STOP ENGAGING EMPLOYEES

Stop Engaging Employees

Start making work more human

ERYC EYL

Chantel Botha

Flourishing Books

CONTENTS

~ 5 ~

Encourage

77

~ 6 ~

Interlude: About generations in the workplace

96

~ 7 ~

Educate

101

~ 8 ~

Interlude: Engage yourself

123

~ 9 ~

Enable

132

~ 10 ~

Interlude: Cultivating a bigger sense of "We"

149

~ 11 ~

Empower

156

~ 12 ~

Interlude: About resistance

169

~ 13 ~

Embrace

176

~ 14 ~

Putting the 6 Es together

192

~ 15 ~

Epilogue and gratitude

203

ADVANCE PRAISE FOR STOP ENGAGING EMPLOYEES

"It's about time someone took a realistic look at cultural experience management! Eryc's insights—not a surprise—are creative, insightful, and refreshing! A great read that is guaranteed to stimulate thought."

—LOU CARBONE, FOUNDER AND CHIEF EXPERIENCE OFFICER, EXPERIENCE ENGINEERING

AUTHOR OF THE AWARD-WINNING BOOK, *CLUED IN: HOW TO KEEP CUSTOMERS COMING BACK AGAIN AND AGAIN*

"Eryc Eyl is right—the war for 'talent' is over. High-performing workplaces must create not only economic value for people but human value."

—DR. PAUL J. ZAK, FOUNDER AND CHIEF IMMERSION OFFICER, IMMERSION NEUROSCIENCE

AUTHOR OF THE AMAZON BEST-SELLING BOOK, *IMMERSION: THE SCIENCE OF THE EXTRAORDINARY AND THE SOURCE OF HAPPINESS*

PREFACE

You are not creating people to be with, or work with, some idealized individuals made of perfect parts of personality that you discovered on your life journey. You are meeting individuals with their own full lives behind and ahead of them. Stop trying to make and fix others, and instead be curious about what they have made of themselves.

ADRIENNE MAREE BROWN, EMERGENT STRATEGY

When I first set out to write this book, I had one question in my mind: Why does work suck? For so many people —of so many different backgrounds, means, privileges, ages, races, genders, sexualities, and abilities—work is nothing more than a four-letter word.

And I think it's because, somewhere along the path of industrialization, financialization, optimization, and automation, we lost our way and forgot this simple truth:

Organizations exist to serve humans, not the other way around.

We humans invented organizations to meet *our* needs, so why have we allowed organizations to bend *us* to serve *their* needs instead?

(And to be clear, by saying this, I don't mean to imply that organizations don't also exist to serve our planet and the other living and non-living beings with whom we share it. I just want to *start* with humanity, because if we don't start there, I think we'll lose the plot—again.)

Inside all organizations are humans. We sometimes call them employees or workers (or team members or associates or partners or...)

Outside all organizations are also humans. We sometimes call them customers or clients (or partners or guests or donors or...)

There are other humans outside of organizations that the organization also serves. These are variously called suppliers, investors, community members, and that most-dreadful of catch-all euphemisms: stakeholders.

All of these humans have needs, aspirations, fears, and motivations. Some are distinct and unique, and most are shared, common, and universal.

When organizations focus on addressing the physical,

psychological, social, and emotional needs of the humans they serve—inside and outside—they increase the likelihood that both the organization and all those humans will achieve what they want to achieve, contribute what they want to contribute, and become what they want to become.

A person's purpose is to be a person. A person's value is in their personhood.

Whether professionally or personally (as if those could be separate things), the purpose of a person isn't to become something else, and it definitely isn't to be an instrument that generates revenue, profits, or productivity.

The purpose of a person is to be the best version of themselves. Now. We need to stop talking about our fellow humans as means to so-called business outcomes (e.g., "happy employees make happy customers," "happy customers make for more-profitable businesses," "healthy cultures make more money," "employee engagement is correlated with higher profitability...").

Business outcomes are just that—outcomes. They are effects. And they happen when people are satisfied, fulfilled, self-actualized, and flourishing.

Human satisfaction, fulfillment, self-actualization, and flourishing are actually the *point* of businesses, and not the other outcomes (which, I get, are much easier to measure).

In our hyper-financialized world, we tend to think of everything in terms of ROI (return on investment, for anyone who doesn't speak Acronymese). But the "return" that matters most is human flourishing.

> *Because children grow up, we think a child's purpose is to grow up. But a child's purpose is to be a child. Nature doesn't disdain what lives only for a day. It pours the whole of itself into each moment. We don't value the lily less for not being made of flint and built to last. Life's bounty is in its flow, later is too late. Where is the song when it's been sung? The dance when it's been danced? It's only we humans who want to own the future, too. We persuade ourselves that the universe is modestly employed in unfolding our destination. ...Was the child happy while he lived? That is a proper question, the only question.*
>
> TOM STOPPARD, THE COAST OF UTOPIA

Too often, humans in management and leadership roles focus on getting their fellow humans in the organization (usually, those with less power) to be different from who they are: be more collaborative, be more compliant, be more efficient, be more productive, be more innovative, be more engaged, be more agile, be more customer-centric, be *more*...

But what *more* would be possible if, instead of focusing on changing other people, we focused on creating the conditions in which they could become the best versions of themselves? Why are we so obsessed with changing people whom we chose to include in our organizations?

This book takes those questions as its inspiration, and offers some concrete and specific advice on how we can approach the possibilities and flourish together in humancentric workplaces that contribute to a more just, equitable, and inclusive world.

INTRODUCTION

I work all day at the factory
I'm building a machine that's not for me
There must be a reason that I can't see
You've got to humanize yourself
THE POLICE "RE-HUMANISE YOURSELF"

Let's start by being honest with each other: sometimes, work just plain sucks. Sometimes, it's nothing more than another four-letter word.

And it's not as fun to say as some of the other ones.

Many years ago, I worked for a large telecommunications company, where I was hired to improve both the customer and the employee experience. But—if I'm honest—what was more important to me at the time was improving my own experience.

This company had a pretty poor reputation as an employer. I'd known people who'd worked there and been miserable, and I'd been warned, but I took a job there because I was desperate. About two years prior, I'd been laid off, and in the intervening years, I'd managed to spend my way through my generous severance.

I was broke.

Truth is, I was more than broke. I'd started working as a coach and consultant but had no idea of how to run a business and no plan for how I would make this work. Not only did I have no money, but I had to borrow thousands of dollars (from my ex-wife if you can believe it) to pay my taxes that year. Talk about a low point.

I admit I wasn't at my best during that particular season of life. Around the time I got laid off from my employer of 10 years, I'd also split up with my wife of 10 years (the afore-mentioned ex-wife). It was definitely the right decision for both of us, but it was still a difficult time. I was rediscovering who I was and who I wanted to be.

A few years before, I'd started freelancing as a music critic, fitting live concerts and interviews into the margins of my corporate life. Now, I was going out to shows four or five times a week—partly because I loved the music, but mostly because I needed to reboot my social life. I started drinking way too much, dating people who weren't good for me, and generally pursuing a pretty self-destructive path. I was in my mid-30s, but living like I was in my early 20s.

I didn't hit rock bottom (though I could hear its siren call from where I was), but I definitely didn't treat my life and the lives of others with the respect and reverence they deserved.

Now, I don't judge anyone who's going through something like that. And I don't judge myself for it either. As dangerous and irresponsible as I was during that short period of my life, I absolutely had to go through that experience to get to where I am now, though I'm deeply sorry for the people I mistreated and hurt as I went through my trainwreck years. I had to drink too much to realize that it only made me feel worse. I had to sleep too little to realize my stupor was affecting my ability to be a good parent to my young daughter. I had to date people who were bad for me to find the love of my life.

And I had to take a job at this terrible company to discover my true contribution to the world. After years of working for a decent employer, I had to experience the opposite to understand more deeply how workplace culture operates, and the power it has to dehumanize and rehumanize.

So there I was: thousands of dollars in debt to my ex-wife, no money coming in, and a young daughter I loved dearly, when an opportunity came up to work for a company I'd heard terrible things about. The pay looked good and I needed *some* kind of stabilizing force in my life, so I took it.

It wasn't long before I realized just how dysfunctional and dehumanizing this particular workplace was.

Most employees didn't speak to each other, unless they worked in the same department or needed something. As I walked through the halls, I'd say hello to people who would avert their eyes in an attempt to avoid connection. I remember one gentleman who visibly flinched when I greeted him with a casual "how's it going" as we passed each other. I was accustomed to connection and community in the workplace, and this felt isolating and sad.

But there was more to this place than just a dearth of friendliness and camaraderie. As was quite common in telecom at the time, this company had acquired several others in a short period of time, thereby gaining miles and miles of network traffic. In the process, the company also acquired a lot of what corporatespeakers like to call "redundant employees." There were more folks in back-office functions like accounting, human resources, information technology, among others, than were necessary to run the rapidly growing company. To deal with this problem while continuing a rapid pace of acquisitions, the company instituted a practice that was both perfectly pragmatic and positively poisonous:

Monthly layoffs.

Yep. On the first Friday of every month, pink slips were distributed to a selection of employees who had been deemed redundant.

Every. Freaken. Month.

And this went on for years. It was a logical, efficient way for the publicly traded company to deal with excess "human capital" and to send savings straight to the bottom line in a way that enticed investors.

Of course, this practice created a sense of scarcity among employees, encouraged internal competition, slowed innovation, and diminished collaboration. It was dehumanizing and eliminated any sense of "we" that might've existed. After all, if I knew there was a chance that one of us—you or I—was going to lose a job at the beginning of the next month, I'd do everything I could to make sure it wasn't me, and I'd focus more on that goal than on doing what I was hired to do—which was simply to help the company attain its vision, fulfill its mission, and achieve its goals.

But it wasn't all bad.

In my previous experience in a high-functioning workplace, I'd learned to view every situation as an opportunity, and this new workplace was, as cynical folks often say, "opportunity-rich." Every time I identified a new problem I thought I could help solve, I pretty much created a new position for myself. In my few years with that company, I managed to invent new jobs and gain the support and sponsorship of some members of the executive team.

One day, I found myself as a guest speaker in the company's professional development program for young leaders. I'd been invited to teach the group about leading and managing organizational change, and I was delighted to see that the company's chief operating officer (COO) had decided to sit in. He was a portly white gentleman in his fifties. Whatever you picture when I say "COO" is at least 90% accurate.

After my session, the whole group sat down to lunch and I found a seat next to the COO. I didn't know him well and thought this might be a good opportunity to better understand his take on corporate culture, organizational effectiveness, and the human side of business.

We exchanged small talk. It was probably about sports, a topic on which I am embarrassingly ignorant, so I worked up the courage to change the subject and ask him the question to which I thought I should already know the answer.

"What's the company's mission?" I asked, kinda out of the blue.

"What do you mean?" he responded reasonably.

"I guess I'm wondering why this company exists. Why do thousands of employees come to work here every day?"

He looked at me, swallowed a mouthful of pasta alfredo, wiped his mouth carefully with a napkin, and said flatly, "We will be a 14-billion-dollar company within the next four years." Then he took another bite.

I didn't know how to respond. It was clear that the COO thought he'd answered my question, but I hadn't received any information close to what I was looking for. I struggled to figure out what to say next.

"I understand that's our financial goal," I said as politely as I could, "and I understand that's what's most important to shareholders, but what about employees? What's the purpose that gets employees out of bed every day?"

This did not go as I'd hoped. It seemed as though something I'd said or the way I'd said it bugged him. He got up from his seat and turned to go. Had I pissed him off? Confused him? Or was he just late for his next meeting? I couldn't tell, but as he was leaving, he looked at me and said, "Employees should get out of bed every day to help make us a 14-billion-dollar company." It wasn't a threat or a declaration. I didn't detect an ounce of emotion in his response; in the worldview to which he'd become accustomed, it was simply true: people existed to serve the organization.

Now, was there anything wrong with what this COO said to me? Maybe not. Maybe what he said is exactly what an executive officer of a publicly traded company within a capitalist economy should say. And maybe he believed it. And maybe there really were some employees who jumped out of bed every morning, excited at the prospect of creating wealth for the company's executives and shareholders.

Maybe.

That conversation was one of a handful of key moments that led to my leaving the company a few months later. Did I mention that work sometimes sucks?

What I've learned in my career, both before and since then, is that most humans are motivated by a purpose beyond profit, and that the purpose needs to be personally meaningful.

Most of us won't get out of bed and spend the majority of our waking hours turning a 12-billion-dollar company into a 14-billion-dollar company, even if we have some way of sharing in that profit. Extrinsic motivators like money, whether for the company or for the individual, can move us and motivate us to expend extra effort in the short term, but they don't create the kind of emotional connection and commitment that ultimately leads to satisfaction, fulfillment, self-actualization, and flourishing.

I've also learned that attempts to motivate people with money go hand-in-hand with other extractive and exploitative business practices (e.g., monthly layoffs) and insidious business jargon like "human resources." They're all part of a dehumanizing approach to business that gets poor results over the long term and negatively impacts society as a whole because, unlike Vegas, what happens at work does *not* stay at work.

But I'm getting ahead of myself. I share this story with you—about some of the darkest days of my adult life, about taking a job out of desperation, and about my experiences in a dehumanizing workplace—because I actually find hope in it. In this story of dehumanization and a lack of human connection are the seeds of what I've come to call humancentric workplaces. Between the lines of this story are the roots of a system and a method for helping all of us become the best versions of ourselves, develop fulfilling connections to our work, and maximize the contribution we make to the world, individually and collectively.

But to get to those roots, we're gonna have to pull some weeds —and we'll start with the problem of "customer-centricity."

Much has been said and written over the past few decades about making workplaces more "customercentric." Management philosophers of various stripes have encouraged organizations to put their customers at the center of their businesses, to obsess over their customers, and even to love their customers. The rationale for this is grounded, almost invariably, in finance. "Companies with better customer experience make more money, save on costs, blah, blah, blah, etc."

But customer-centricity can be just as extractive as profit-centricity. You don't have to look hard to find countless "customercentric" organizations that exploit, mistreat, and exhaust their employees in the name of putting the customer first. It's not only an unsustainable way to run a business; it's inhumane.

And then there's the problem of "employee-centricity": organizations putting their employees at the center of their businesses, putting employees first, and even loving their employees. This sounds pretty good except, once again, the rationale had to include units of currency, like the cost of employee turnover or the cost of lost productivity. "Happy employees make happy customers and happy customers spend more money, blah, blah, barf."

As with most dichotomies, the true path is both and neither. Organizations that choose to focus on customers or employees miss the point. In fact, it's impossible to be "customercentric" or "employee-centric" unless one is, first, humancentric. In my years of working in and with organizations, I've found that humancentric workplaces—places where work is more than just a four-letter word—get better results for their customers, their employees, their suppliers, their shareholders, and their communities. These workplaces focus on addressing the needs, aspirations, fears, and motivations of all the humans they touch. And the so-called "business results" take care of themselves.

In parallel with all the talk of customercentricity and employeecentricity has been a great deal of talk about automation and artificial intelligence. Every week, it seems there's a new insight about how humans are being removed from value creation, replaced by algorithms and automatons. We're told that ChatXYZ is going to replace doctors, lawyers, waitstaff, auto mechanics, and rappers.

But removing human effort from work isn't new. Ever since the first industrial revolution, we've made strides toward taking work out of human hands and giving it to machines. As we've done so, the nature of work done by humans has changed. Way back in the 20th century, Peter Drucker coined the term "knowledge worker" because, weirdly and suddenly, humans were suddenly valued as much for their brains as for their ability to imitate machines.

Since then, we've eliminated, outsourced, and automated much of the work (even the so-called "knowledge work") required to bring products and services to market. And while that can cause our lizard brains to freak out a little bit (we *do* hate to lose things), what it actually means is that the work left for us humans is seriously valuable. Rather than making us less important, the evolution of technology has made all of us *more* important. Cool, right?

So it's not the technology that's dehumanizing us; it's ourselves. When we talk about maximizing shareholder value or driving productivity or even putting the customer first, we're diminishing our own inherent value as humans and subjugating ourselves as instruments to serve financial ends, rather than as beautiful, perfect ends in ourselves.

In today's economy, value is often created when humans interact. Whether it's employees interacting with their colleagues, employees serving customers, or even customers serving fellow customers, value creation depends on human interactions—over a service counter, over Slack, in a warehouse, or on a manufacturing floor. Many of us in the modern economy have evolved from knowledge workers to interaction workers, and this evolution makes humancentric workplaces a *business* imperative.

What's more, we spend so much time working, and as has been articulated in psychological research, what we experience at work crosses over into other areas of our lives, and spills over onto the friends and family that we hold most dear. So what we experience at work doesn't just affect ourselves and our organizations, but also the larger communities and societies in which we live. For that reason, creating humancentric workplaces is also a *moral* imperative.

Finally, as we noted earlier, we humans do *not* exist to serve organizations. In our collective brilliance, we *created* organizations to serve *us*. When we realized that we couldn't survive as solitary units, that we could accomplish more together than alone, and that we're interdependent by nature, we invented organizations that could help us meet our needs, pursue our aspirations, quell our fears, and nurture our motivations. Those organizations make stuff for us, like pizza rolls and electric cars. They also employ us, giving us opportunities to make meaningful contributions to the world while keeping ourselves fed, clothed, and housed. And they give back to their communities, helping us all grow and stay alive. In this way, humancentric workplaces are simply a *survival* imperative.

A humancentric workplace is built around human needs —physiological, psychological, social, and emotional. It's a workplace in which we humans can make awesome contributions and become the best versions of ourselves, and it contributes to a more just, equitable, and inclusive world. It prioritizes those needs—along with our aspirations, fears, and motivations—and knows that traditional business outcomes (e.g., profits) are just lagging indicators that they're handling those priorities well.

We could call this kind of workplace, in which human flourishing is the primary goal, not just humancentric, but *humanitarian*, and it contrasts pretty starkly with the traditional view of workplaces that treat humans as a means to financial ends. We could call that kind of workplace *instrumentarian.*

In the difference between an *instrumentarian* orientation to work and a *humanitarian* orientation to work lies the difference between subjugation and liberation. If we proceed under the mistaken notion that humans exist to achieve financial outcomes, we limit what we and our fellow humans can contribute and become in this world. That's the instrumentarian approach.

If, on the other hand, we proceed with the assumption that humans exist to seek happiness, satisfaction, fulfillment, and flourishing—something like the state of eudaimonia espoused in ancient Greek ethics—then we create room for the infinite gifts, contributions, cogitations, and capabilities of our fellow humans. That's the humanitarian approach.

My hope, in writing this book, is to provide both inspiration and instruction to stop treating customers and employees as anything less than they are: our fellow humans. We can create greater value, build healthier communities, take better care of our planet, and increase justice and equity in our world by building workplaces that put human needs, aspirations, fears, and motivations at the center.

In this book, we'll explore what's gone wrong with most organizations, and why it's time to develop a more human-centric approach to work and business. I'll explain why the typical approaches to employee engagement haven't accomplished much of anything, and why we urgently need new approaches to achieve better business and societal outcomes.

But we'll spend most of our time together focused on how to create humancentric workplaces and businesses. We'll use the "6 Es" framework as a lens through which to view how we humans engage with our work. And we'll learn from real-world examples of companies that have attempted to treat their employees as more than a means of production and their customers as more than consumers.

Throughout the book, we'll take steps together to make sure we're ready to turn the ideas and frameworks in these pages into actions that will make our workplaces more humancentric, regardless of where we work in the organization.

I like to think of any book as a contract between author and reader. As part of that contract, I make three commitments to you as the author:

- **I'll provide practical recommendations, grounded in consistent philosophical principles.** While I consider myself a management philosopher, I know the day-to-day realities of working in and running a business. Philosophy is, simply, a love of wisdom, but I will ground that wisdom in reality and use it to provide practical advice you can implement immediately.

- **I won't pad the book with extra pages.** In my opinion, most contemporary business books are about two times longer than they need to be. I will include as much information as I think will be practical and useful to you, but I won't add extraneous content just to make it look bigger, justify a higher cover price, and give it an ego-feeding "thud" factor.

- **I won't bullshit you.** This one should go without saying, but I want you to know that I take your time and your success seriously. While writing this book, I took inspiration from Josh Bernoff's *Writing Without Bullshit* to make sure I stuck to the point. This means you won't find a ton of extra citations or references to make myself sound smart. I'm far more interested in helping you than impressing you. You will, however, find a list of books, articles, ideas, and people that have informed my thinking at the back of this book, so that you can do more research, if you're into that kind of thing.

Oh, and the elephant in the room: why have I titled this book *Stop Engaging Employees*? Am I suggesting that employee engagement is a bad thing, that employers shouldn't worry about engaged employees, that all this "employee-first" business should stop?

Absolutely not. In fact, quite the opposite of all those things, but with some key adjustments:

- Employee engagement is a good and necessary thing for successful organizations, but the way we've been thinking about it and doing it is all wrong.
- Employers should worry about engaged employees, but they should stop looking at engagement as something they can or should do *to employees*
- Employers should put employees first, but they should stop thinking of us as "employees," and start thinking of us as "fellow humans."
- We are not cultivating engaged employees so that we can achieve financial outcomes. Instead, we are pursuing engagement for ourselves and others so that we can be fully human.

We'll get into the details of all this in the following chapters, but for now, just know that *Stop Engaging Employees* is a plea and a plan to start doing business in a way that gets better outcomes for all the humans involved, and it's based on 13 key principles.

If you're reading this book in paper form, you might want to dog-ear this section so you can come back to it when you need to fortify your resolve to become a humancentric leader.

The 13 guiding principles of humancentric workplaces

These principles are presented in no particular order because I believe each item is equal to the others; there is no hierarchy among these principles. Like the rest of this book, this list isn't "done" yet; I reserve the right to review, revise, and even contradict these guiding principles as I learn more. Still, my hope is that these guiding principles provide fertile soil to cultivate workplaces that are more human.

While you can fly through this list of principles in just a few minutes, I encourage you to pause and reflect on each principle. What does it really mean? How does it challenge assumptions you've long held? What would be different if you let it guide your approach to work and life? Take your time. Question. Philosophize. Scribble notes in the margins. Don't just read the words—engage with them.

Each guiding principle is presented in an "X>Y" format (for those of you who slept through math class [no shame or shade meant], that means "X is greater than Y"). This approach makes sense to me because we're not declaring that Y isn't important or isn't necessary or should be banished forever to an island with no WiFi and "Baby Shark" playing on repeat. Instead, I'm merely saying that X is more important, more powerful, more empowering, and more worthy of our limited and ever-endangered focus.

So let's go.

POSSIBILITIES > PROBLEMS

Humancentric workplaces develop the ability to see what's truly possible. Sure, we sometimes have to solve problems, but we need to stay focused on vividly conceiving and pursuing new possibilities that go beyond "fixing" the current state. We can't build new highways to new destinations if all we're doing is repairing potholes.

INVOLVEMENT > INSTRUCTION

Organizations that aren't humancentric think that positive change happens when you teach people new information. Humancentric workplaces know that change isn't real until our fellow humans do things differently, and we're more likely to do things differently when we're part of creating the change. As Meg Wheatley correctly observed, we all support what we help to create. Sometimes change requires acquiring new knowledge or skills, but we should start by involving as many of our fellow humans as we can in co-creating the future we hope they'll embrace.

CONNECTION > COMPLIANCE

When humans connect in meaningful ways, we create new possibilities and stronger, more resilient communities. The power of authentic connections far exceeds what can be accomplished by simply getting so-called employees to comply with new rules, policies, or procedures.

CLARITY > CLEVERNESS

Don't get me wrong—I love brilliant ideas, playful puns, lilting alliteration, and egregious assonance. But I also know that attempts to be clever can often confuse and constrain where clarity can ignite and inspire positive change.

STRENGTHS > WEAKNESSES

Every person and every organization has strengths that contain their potential to make awesome contributions to their customers, families, friends, and communities. We should work to uncover those strengths and build on them. They're more important to the organization's future than any weaknesses that exist.

INTRINSIC > EXTRINSIC

Extrinsic motivators can get us to do things we don't want to do—for a little while, at least. That's why, after I make this dentist appointment I've been dreading, I'm going to enjoy a fistful of gummy bears. But gummy bears will never make me love dentist appointments as much as I love, say, listening to very loud heavy metal (which is to say: a lot). When we feel emotionally connected and committed to what we do (i.e., intrinsically instead of extrinsically motivated), we do whatever it is better.

WHY > WHAT

We'll come back to this one over and over. When all members of a team or organization understand why we're doing whatever we're doing, we often create better ways to do it. When circumstances require a focus on *what*, as they sometimes do, we should focus on putting that *what* into a broader context that we all can easily understand and support.

AUTHENTICITY > AUTHORITY

When leaders like us—whether formal or informal—show up as our whole selves, we create powerful connections, inspire action, and teach others that authenticity is a superpower that far exceeds the power that comes with hierarchies and titles.

HUMANS > EMPLOYEES

When humans interact with an organization—as employees or customers—we don't stop being humans. In the quest to make a positive impact on work and the world, I prefer harnessing the power of my fellow humans—who are capable of literally almost anything—to directing and controlling the actions of "employees." or "customers." In fact, I don't really even like the word "harnessing."

LISTENING > TALKING

When we listen to one another, we create connections, trust, and relationships that make us capable of more. The best leaders know how to ask questions and listen to the answers.

CONSISTENCY > INTENSITY

I'm indebted to Simon Sinek for giving me the words for this principle, though I'm pretty sure he got the idea from someone else. We develop more constructive and powerful beliefs when we consistently experience and learn that we're *expected* to be constructive and powerful. A single training class or well-worded poster won't do it, but consistent, intentional experiences over time will. It's easy to put an event—like a team-building session or a holiday party—on the calendar, but that doesn't mean the event really *did* anything.

LOVE > FEAR

When we feel that an organization and its leaders care about us, can help us, and can be trusted, we become capable of more than even *we* thought was possible. The potential of love to ignite and inspire is far stronger than the power that fear has to compel and control.

WE > THEY

What we mean when we say "We" makes all the difference in what we're capable of accomplishing, and what we need now, more than ever, is a bigger, broader sense of "We." When our "We" is small, and includes just those we work closely with, or just those who we perceive to be most like us, our potential is correspondingly small. But when we broaden our sense of "We," we expand what's possible. This one is so important that it'll get its own chapter later in the book.

These 13 guiding principles provide the fertile soil in which humancentric workplaces can grow and flourish. Whether you're an entry-level employee, a veteran middle manager, or a seasoned senior leader, you have the power to make your workplace more humancentric. Your mindset, attitudes, and behaviors can and will make a difference. The rest of this book will provide you with the disciplines to practice, while these guiding principles provide you with the solid ground to stand on while you practice.

WHY SHOULD YOU LISTEN TO ME?

O h, man. Many people have told me I need to include this chapter in my book, a chapter that tells you why I'm an expert in this field, why my perspective matters, what my credentials are, and, in short, who the hell I think I am.

And I get it. I mean, there are a *lot* of books out there and your time is precious, so you shouldn't waste time with books by people you shouldn't listen to. So I'll indulge the question, "Why should I listen to you?" but I'm also going to subvert it—partly because I think it's a problematic question, and partly because I'm just that much of an unrepentant contrarian punk.

About me

I've spent roughly three decades working in and with corporate organizations in the for-profit and nonprofit worlds. During that time, I've worked in many different parts of the business: manufacturing, customer service, marketing, purchasing, IT, quality, training and development, finance, sales, business process management, and research. I've also worked as an executive coach, work-life balance coach, change management consultant, facilitator, organizational effectiveness consultant, and consultant on workplace culture and employee engagement. I've held jobs responsible for employee communication, employee engagement, change management, and customer experience. I've led keynote sessions, breakouts, and workshops on customer experience, change management, corporate culture, team effectiveness, leadership, and employee engagement at various conferences and corporate events, as well as for private clients. These days, I spend most of my time speaking, writing, and advising on topics that relate to humancentric workplaces.

As for credentials, I have a few. My graduate degree is in secondary education (I once thought I'd be a high school English teacher, but then thought better of it), which is actually highly relevant to the ideas within this book. I was certified by General Electric (a company that, despite its significant shortcomings, helped shape and launch my career) as a Six Sigma Black Belt, which is a fancy way of saying I know something about analyzing data to improve business processes. Prosci, the leading research and training organization for change management, certified me as a practitioner of their tools and methods. I'm certified by Human Synergistics to administer and apply the Organizational Culture Inventory and Organizational Effectiveness Inventory, which are tools I use in my consulting work for rigorous assessment of workplace cultures. I'm also certified to use the DISC assessment (a tool for understanding and adjusting the ways we interact with other people), and I received certification from the

Association of Training and Development in the Phillips ROI methodology (see the Educate chapter for more on that). The Customer Experience Professionals Association has granted me the Certified Customer Experience Professional designation, and I've served as a judge for the North American Customer Centricity Awards and the Customer Centricity World Series. I swear I'm not making any of this stuff up, but it kinda sounds silly when I write it all down.

Of course, you could learn pretty much all of that stuff from my CV or LinkedIn profile. But if I were to review your CV or LinkedIn profile, would I really know who you are? Probably not.

Your credentials don't define you, nor do mine. In addition to all that fancy stuff, I've spent years as a professional music journalist and DJ. I'm also a husband, father, brother, son, neighbor, activist, storyteller, and playwright. I used to be a pretty good jazz trumpet player, and now I'm a hack on the ukulele. I'm a decent-but-infrequent cook and baker. I've recently learned how to freestyle rap. Oh, and I'm frequently plagued by self-doubt, shyness, self-consciousness, and defensiveness. How about you?

I am, at my core, a philosopher and educator. I love—and fancy that I'm good at—pondering big ideas and connecting the dots between seemingly unrelated disciplines. I also love, and think I'm pretty good at, facilitating learning for others, which I do through my coaching, consulting, speaking, and writing.

I fundamentally believe that the key to making the world better for all humans is to let loose the enormous power of individual agency for collective good. We're all in this together, but we're only as strong as the least of us. When we do this "being human" thing right, we make each other smarter, stronger, more resilient, and happier.

So why, again, should you listen to me?

I'm afraid the foregoing doesn't make a particularly strong case for why you should listen to me, but I hope that it, at least, helps you decide whether you *want* to listen to me or not. I'm not here to convince you I'm an expert or a "thought leader." I'm not even sure either of those things really exists. But I've spent a lot of time thinking about and applying the ideas in this book, and I believe they can improve the world of work and, by extension, the world.

And I've also made a *ton* of mistakes on the way to these pages. As you read this book, I'll share some of the approaches and tactics that have worked for me, but believe me when I tell you that I've crashed and burned a million times. For real. I've really screwed up. And I invite you to do the same. This mission of improving the human experience of work is not an exact science. It requires experimentation, and experimentation requires failure. So while this book will provide you lots of support and allow you to avoid the mistakes I've made, just know that you'll make your own mistakes, and that's just a sign that you're doing the work. Take risks, with love and concern for your fellow humans in your heart. When you screw up, as I have, heal the harm, repair the relationships, and move forward a little better. I'll be here, cheering you on.

I believe work can be more than just another four-letter word. In fact, I believe it can be a meaningful path toward satisfaction, fulfillment, self-actualization, and flourishing for all of us. And I believe that workplaces and business can do more than just extract value from humans and other natural resources. In fact, I believe they can contribute to a just, equitable, and inclusive world.

And I don't think I'm alone. The more people I talk to, the more I'm convinced that there's a movement afoot—that there are dozens, thousands, millions of us who believe that the future of work won't and shouldn't look like the past—that we can rediscover the fundamentally human activity of work and fundamentally transform workplaces. If that sounds like something that might interest you, I'd be honored if you joined the movement. Let's stop engaging employees, and start making work more human.

~ 1 ~

WHAT'S WRONG WITH
ENGAGING EMPLOYEES?

"We are caught in an inescapable network of
mutuality, tied in a single garment of destiny. What-
ever affects one directly, affects all indirectly."
MARTIN LUTHER KING, JR. WHY WE CAN'T
WAIT

S o why should we stop engaging employees? One word:
grammar.

Ok, it's definitely more than just that one word, but grammar
is a good place to start.

Now, wait. Before your middle-school flashbacks cause you to
slam this book shut, let me make this as painless as possible.

Let's take a simple sentence that is the opposite of the title
of this book: "The organization engages employees."

In that sentence, who is doing what to whom? It's pretty straightforward, right? The subject of the sentence (the organization) are doing a verb (engage) to an object (employees). Yes, I just called employees "objects." Dehumanization sneaks up on you sometimes.

But this isn't really how it works, is it? Engagement is a condition that we, as humans, develop—like love, or plantar fasciitis. No one does it *to us*. When we engage, we connect and commit—to our work, to our purpose, and sometimes even to the organization. We aren't the *object*; the object is the work, our purpose, and the organization.

Put simply: *We* are the *subject* of the employee engagement sentence.

So the more-accurate sentence is: "Employees engage with the organization."

But that's not the way it's been viewed over the past few decades.

A little history of the employee engagement industrial complex

The trouble is that if we accept that employees are the subject and we can't do engagement *to* them, we can't sell all the interventions—assessments, software, training, posters, playing cards, stress balls, air fresheners—that claim to engage employees and make employees the object of the sentence.

Since the term was introduced by William Kahn in 1990, a huge industry has grown up around "employee engagement." There are employee engagement vendors focused on employee listening, on wellbeing, on training, and on recognition. They offer surveys to measure it, software platforms to manage it, and consultants to increase it. And that's before you get into the even more cluttered and confusing market of "employee experience," where project management platforms, scheduling systems, intranets, collaboration tools, and a gazillion other technologies collide in a desperate clamor for a share of growing budgets.

But that's a whole other book (I'll say that a lot, but only because I want to keep this book short). For now, let's just focus on the industry that is organized around the seemingly altruistic goal of increasing employee engagement.

Employee engagement is big business. In 2012, Bersin and Associates found global spending on employee engagement to be around 720 million US dollars. According to a report from Future Market Insights, the total global market for employee engagement had more than doubled by 2022, reaching $1.6 billion. That same report estimated that the market would reach $3.8 billion by 2032. Holy crap! That's a lot of money, right? I mean, that's *billions* of dollars!

So what are we getting for our money?

Well, if you look at the most-popular benchmarks of employee engagement, you're likely to come to a simple conclusion: diddly squat. To avoid some strange statistical anomalies, let's start by looking at data from prior to COVID-19.

Before we do, I just want to make something clear. This isn't the kind of business book that tries to impress or bore you with a bunch of statistics. This is a book about humans, and as the saying goes, statistics are humans with the tears dried off. But a little bit of data upfront will give us some helpful context.

A short data detour

Data from Gallup, Inc. State of the Global Workplace 2023 report. Go to
Gallup.com for more information.
Illustration by Chantel Botha

In February 2020, the Gallup organization, which probably
has the largest data set on employee engagement around
the world, reported seemingly remarkable findings. After 20
years of measuring this important business outcome, the percentage of engaged employees in the United States reached
a new high of 35% in 2019. While that's not a particularly
impressive number, it had climbed nine percentage points
since 2000.

Gallup has tracked employee engagement across a broad
swath of US organizations since 2000. In that first year, Gallup

estimated that 26% of US employees were engaged, while 18% were actively disengaged. In the middle of 2021, 36% of employees were engaged—the largest percentage so far—and 15% were actively disengaged. But by the end of 2022, just 33% of employees were engaged (the lowest number since 2017), and fully 18% were actively disengaged (the same percentage as in 2000).

Still, 33% engaged in 2022 is inarguably better than 26% in 2000, so there's some improvement, right? But with billions of dollars spent 2000, wouldn't you expect more?

In fact, the lack of improvement is the real story in Gallup's data, and that becomes even clearer when we look at the remaining 49% of US employees, who we will get to in a second. But first, let's zoom out from the US to the whole world.

On a global scale, Gallup doesn't have as many years of data, but it tells a similar story. In 2022, the percentage of global employees that Gallup calls "actively disengaged" was 18%, the same as in the US, while the percentage "engaged" reached a dismal high of 23%, the highest percentage seen since Gallup began tracking global numbers in 2009 (at which time, the percentage engaged was 12%, with 27% actively disengaged). Is this progress? Maybe. But 59% of 2022's global employees are still unaccounted for. Don't worry; we're getting there.

To better understand these data, it helps to know how Gallup defines three categories of employees:

- **Engaged.** "Involved in and enthusiastic" about the work they do, these folks willingly expend "discretionary effort" to help their organizations achieve their goals. For example, they're more likely to take proactive steps to improve customer service, address problems, and take advantage of opportunities to make the organization more successful. Again, this was 1 out of 3 folks in the US and less than 1 out of 4 globally in 2022.

- **Actively disengaged.** The smallest group, these folks are emotionally disconnected from their work and workplace. They negatively impact performance and can even undermine their organizations' strategies. This was slightly less than 1 in 5 employees in the US and around the world in 2022.

- **Not engaged.** This is the largest group in Gallup's historical data, but they rarely explicitly report it or analyze it. Why is that? While these folks—49% in the US, 59% globally in 2022—might be "satisfied" with their work, they lack the emotional connection and commitment that enables them to make awesome contributions and become the best versions of themselves through their work.

If we revisit the data above with these definitions in mind, there are a few things to home in on:

- The percentage of employees who are "involved and enthusiastic" has increased by just 7 percentage points in the US in 22 years and 11 percentage points globally in 13 years. What's more, this increase has had its ups and downs, so it's a little soon to call it a trend.

- The percentage of employees whose disengagement is destructive (i.e., the "actively disengaged") is the same in the US today as it was in 2000. Globally, it has dropped 9 percentage points in 13 years.

- The percentage of employees who are satisfied but not truly engaged (which Gallup tellingly labels "not engaged") has decreased nonlinearly in the US over 22 years by only 7 percentage points. At the global level, it has decreased 2 percentage points since 2009. This group of our fellow humans—49% of us in the US, 59% of us worldwide—appears to have been the least impacted by the employee engagement industrial complex over the years. This rarely reported statistic *should* be grabbing all the headlines. Nearly 6 out of 10 employees globally were not engaged in 2022.

Since we don't have access to Gallup's data, we can't do any really nerdy/fun stuff like testing the differences throughout the years for statistical significance, or examining the (most likely highly significant) differences by race or gender or ability or age, but I'm not a statistician, and this ain't that kind of book anyway. However, in practical terms, we can see that engagement, especially as measured by the percentage "not engaged," has remained flat over two decades, even while big bucks have been spent.

Can you think of any other key performance indicator in business that would continue to receive that much investment while remaining, essentially, unchanged? One business leader I spoke with suggested that maybe this level of investment was necessary to just keep the number flat, and that any less investment in employee engagement would result in a decline. I guess that could be. But if that's true, what the hell? What would that tell us about the nature of our workplaces? Either way, given the apparent return on this sizable investment, is it possible—just possible—that we're doing it all wrong?

What the heck is employee engagement?

If you're going to try to change something, or even just try to measure it, it helps to have a clear definition of what, exactly, it is.

In 1990, William Kahn, a professor of management and organizations at Boston University, started the modern conversation about employee engagement with an article titled, "Psychological Conditions of Personal Engagement and Disengagement at Work." Behind that sexy, clickbait-worthy title, Kahn defined engagement as a condition in which people were "harnessed" to their work roles and expressed themselves physically, cognitively, and emotionally as they did their jobs. Disengaged folks, on the other hand, "uncoupled" themselves from their work, withdrew, and defended themselves. I don't know what to do with this whole idea of being "harnessed" like livestock, but to keep this book brief, I'll let it go for now.

You can see pretty clearly how this influenced Gallup's definitions with ideas like being "involved in and enthusiastic" about work vs. "emotionally disconnected." But not everyone sees it the same way. Research from ADP, a global provider of outsourced HR services, refers to "productivity" and "intention to stay" as indicators of employee engagement. When other big players talk about the term, some equate it with "happiness" and "satisfaction," while others use terms like "commitment," "motivation," and "morale." In short, it's a mess. And that mess matters.

Think about it this way. Let's say you and I, along with two other friends, are going to meet for a fun week of sightseeing in glorious Granada. We all agree that April looks good, and we set off independently to plan our trip.

When April comes, I'm so excited. I board my flight in the morning and, later that day, arrive in the gorgeous colonial city of Granada, Nicaragua. Unfortunately, you made completely different plans, and I find myself alone. You're getting your bearings in Granada, Spain, while our two friends are settling into Airbnbs in Granada, Peru, and Granada, Colorado. We all went to Granada, but we're pretty far from what we'd set out to accomplish.

Employee engagement is like Granada. It's the destination we all reached, but we all ended up in different places.

Or, more precisely, it's how we *feel* when we're in Granada. It's the emotional connection and commitment we feel to Granada, created by the sights, sounds, tastes, smells, interactions, and experiences we encounter.

In other words, employee engagement is a destination, an outcome of a bunch of other factors, and when we try to improve employee engagement without understanding and improving those factors—and without agreeing on the destination—the best we can hope for is superficial improvement. The more-likely scenario is that we don't really improve anything. We spend, say, 1.6 *billion* US dollars to keep the metric more or less flat and enjoy our parallel vacations in our own separate Granadas.

I think we can do better. And I'm hoping that the ideas in this book help with that. Let's start with a clear, concise definition, and let's get really specific. Rather than homing in on an abstract concept like "employee engagement," though, let's get even more human and define an engaged employee.

For the purposes of this book, and for our shared understanding of both Granada and what it feels like to be there, an engaged employee is

a fellow human who is so emotionally connected
and committed to their work that they willingly
and proactively go above and beyond their job
description to help the organization attain its
vision, fulfill its mission, and achieve its goals in
return for the promise of increased satisfaction,
fulfillment, self-actualization, and flourishing

That's about 50 words, which is pretty concise, without sacrificing clarity. To broaden and deepen our shared understanding of what we'll be setting out to accomplish in the rest of this book, let's examine the key components of this definition.

- **A fellow human.** This is not inconsequential. To pursue this goal with authenticity, integrity, respect, and humancentricity (a word I'll use throughout this book to refer to the notion that the nucleus of all human organizations, around which all else spins, is a group of humans, some of whom are employees, some of whom are customers, and all of whom are people), we need to recognize these humans as no different or separate from ourselves. Words like "employee" and "customer" tend to objectify and dehumanize, putting our fellow humans into convenient, reductive boxes, and conceiving of them as instruments for achieving other (usually financial) goals. When we recognize their humanity, we have to embrace their complexity and individuality, and realize that we can't treat them as a homogeneous group of objects to be manipulated.

- **Emotionally connected and committed to their work.** Four important concepts are contained here:
  1. Engagement is *emotional,* which means it isn't rational. That will become important when we start talking about what works to cultivate it, and what doesn't.
  2. Engagement is about connection, which means that the engaged human feels as if their life—the stuff they really care about, like their life's mission or vision or goals—are somehow attached to the organization (but let's not say "harnessed," ok?).
  3. The engaged human also feels committed, which implies a sense of bind or obligation. This component connects our definition to the etymology of "engagement," which we can trace back to an Old French term that means "under pledge." There's an implication of loyalty there, but not to any specific organization or person; it's loyalty to a cause or a purpose.
  4. All this connection and commitment relates to something very specific: our work. In other words, "engagement" isn't just an abstract state, but a transitive one that joins us to our work, which includes not only what we do, but also where we do it, why we do it, and with whom (and, as we'll discuss later, "work" and "job" are

not interchangeable ideas here). Before continuing with this book, it'll be helpful for you to determine just what exactly you want employees to engage with. In most cases, it's your top strategic priority, but it might also be with an aspirational culture or a result your organization needs to achieve. Whatever it is, absolute clarity on what you want your fellow humans to engage *with* is a necessary precondition to cultivating that thing called employee engagement. Otherwise, "engagement" remains a squishy state of existence, and we can't have that.

- **Willingly and proactively go above and beyond.** Again, there's a fair amount to unpack in this phrase, but it can be distilled to this: an engaged human does more than expected, gladly and without being asked. That means they'll contribute more to the organization than is expected, and they'll probably do it before anyone thinks to tell them to do it. While doing so, they'll stretch beyond their own limits and grow. This is *not* about the organization trying to extract more from the individual, or about the individual overextending and burning out. Engaged humans do this because doing work that matters to them is fulfilling as part of their journey toward being the best version of themselves. We'll explore that further in just a sec.

- **To help the organization attain its vision, fulfill its mission, and achieve its goals.** When we say, "vision, mission, goals," what we're really saying is, "all the stuff that's most important to the organization" or "pretty much the whole reason the organization exists." As above, this component of the definition answers the unasked question: engagement with what?

- **In return for the promise of increased satisfaction, fulfillment, self-actualization, and flourishing.** Here, we really unpack the fact that the organization isn't extracting uncompensated value from the humans who make it run. For too long, we've talked about people going "above and beyond" without compensation, but the compensation that we all receive for our efforts is the *promise* (i.e., not the guarantee) of increased satisfaction (having our needs met), fulfillment (nourishing our hearts, minds, and souls), self-actualization (becoming the best versions of ourselves), and flourishing (existing in a situation in which we continue to grow and thrive).

There we have it. Let's say it again, just to make sure we're crystal clear.

An engaged employee is a fellow human who is so emotionally connected and committed to their work that they willingly and proactively go above and beyond their job description to help the organization attain its vision, fulfill its mission, and achieve its goals in return for the promise of increased satisfaction, fulfillment, self-actualization, and flourishing

The inner game of engagement

While helping the organization attain its vision, fulfill its mission, and achieve its goals is important, and provides a solid "business case" for employee engagement, there's also something a little more complex happening here.

The engaged human isn't selflessly in service to the organization; they're a complex, autonomous individual with a unique combination of needs, motivations, fears, and aspirations. They come from different backgrounds of ability and disability, race and ethnicity, gender and sexuality, privilege and privation. And when they experience this thing called engagement with their work, they also gain greater access to their own potential. In this way, engagement is a superpower that enables engaged humans to do two important things:

- Make awesome, meaningful contributions that enable the organization to do and accomplish things it couldn't otherwise

- Become the best, highest version of themselves (to "self-actualize," if you speak Maslovian)

When this happens, work transcends its mundane existence as just another four-letter word to be minimized in our lives, and instead becomes a path toward self-actualization and a better world. That's the *real* reason why all this stuff matters.

Stop doing engagement *to employees*

With our 50-word definition in mind, I hope it's becoming clear why the traditional approaches to employee engagement aren't getting results. Contemplate the definition again and you'll see that surveying your fellow humans won't accomplish that. Communication won't. Giving people raises or bonuses won't accomplish that. Training won't do it, nor will "perks and bennies."

While some of those tactics might be helpful when combined with a humancentric philosophy and approach, on their own, they amount to doing engagement *to employees.*

It's like the Crusades. The organization is the religion and employees are the target population to be manipulated (or brutalized) into adopting that religion. We begin to see why dehumanizing language ("workforce," "labor," "human capital," etc.) is integral to the old approaches. If our fellow humans are "resources" who need "upskilling," they can quickly become commodities to be exploited, traded, or discarded. Ah, layoffs!

To take our ridiculous Crusades analogy further, the surveys, communication campaigns, raises, bonuses, training, perquisites, and benefits are the swords that the Crusaders used to gain "converts." Steering clear of the theology here, do you think those "converts" were "emotionally connected and committed" to their new religion, or were they simply trying not to get brutally murdered?

Here's the hard truth. Just as with religion, "true believers" within organizations aren't coerced or convinced; at some point, they make a choice or develop a condition called "true belief." Coercion and convincing—the hallmarks of so many well-intended employee engagement efforts—are good at getting compliance and conformity, especially in the short term. But true emotional connection and commitment come from within, and the best that a leader with integrity can do is support and co-create the conditions in which that kind of connection and commitment can flourish. They'll also respect those among their fellow humans who just aren't feeling it. These leaders—official and unofficial—stop doing engagement *to employees* and start doing engagement *with employees.* That's what the rest of this book is all about.

What doesn't work to cultivate engagement

And yet, the usual approaches to "engaging employees" persist in viewing employees as a target in need of some kind of intervention. The way I see it, there are three basic ways we typically go about trying to engage our fellow humans:

- **Broadcast.** We *tell* people all about what they're supposed to engage with.
- **Bribe.** We provide *incentives* for people to engage.
- **Berate.** We *order* people to engage.

Let's look at the **broadcast** method first. The age-old theory here is: if we give people enough information, they'll develop an emotional connection and commitment that changes their mindsets, attitudes, and behaviors. Essentially, we just have to convince our fellow humans of the brilliance of our vision or strategy or approach, and they'll accept and adopt it. It's as if we believe we can *tell* our way to transformation. This assumes that people, when presented with enough of the right information, will do what we want them to do. If this were true, the world would be a very simple (and boring) place. Information and communication are important, but we humans derive much more information from what an organization and its leaders do than from what they say.

Next is the **bribe** method. The theory here is: if we promise to give our fellow humans something they want, they'll develop an emotional connection and commitment that changes their mindsets, attitudes, and behaviors. This assumes that people are mechanistic and will do what we want them to do when they get the right bribe. There's nothing wrong with the judicious use of incentives as part of a holistic approach to cultivating engagement. On its own, however, this approach robs people (and their employers) of their agency and self-efficacy, while sending the message that whatever they're being asked to swallow requires a spoonful of sugar to be palatable and isn't sufficient on its own. In other words, if it was really desirable, you wouldn't have to bribe me to go along with it.

The last of the usual approaches is the **berate** method. The theory here is that our fellow humans simply need to be told what to do. Cultivating engagement is as easy as giving commands. Unfortunately, for leaders who buy into this, command does not always lead to control. Instead, it leads to passivity, groupthink, and dependence. It's a good recipe for conformity and compliance, especially in the short term, but it won't lead to an authentic connection and commitment.

All three of these methods basically mean you're *doing* engagement *to* your fellow humans, that your vision is being *inflicted* upon others.

And let's be real: when we do things *to people*, they don't tend to like it. Engaging employees—that is, cultivating an emotional connection and commitment—creates change in an organization and in the humans inside it. And because **broadcast, bribe, and berate** are the usual approaches, we start to think that people are naturally resistant—to engagement, to work, and to change.

But when you think about it, we humans willingly invite and pursue change in our lives all the time. That change might be a new car, a new phone, a new haircut, or new biceps. But the point is, we aren't actually inherently averse to change. In fact, Peter Senge, an expert in social systems and organizational learning, teaches us: "People don't resist change. We resist being changed."

Doing engagement *with employees*

If we want our visions of a sugar-plum future to come to life, then, as much as possible, we need to pursue those visions *with* the humans who engage, and avoid doing our visions *to them.*

If we can cultivate a humancentric workplace *with* our fellow humans, we're more likely to gain the kind of emotional connection and commitment we need to not just make change, but to sustain it and get the awesome results that authentic engagement can bring, all while bringing out the best in our fellow humans.

To create a lasting humancentric workplace, we need more than the compliance and conformity we get through **broadcast, bribing, and berating**. We need people to be as invested in the success of our vision as we are. We need authentic connection and commitment, and that goes beyond just convincing people it's a good idea with information, bribing them to come along with us, or just telling them what to do.

Of course, we also have to acknowledge that not all of our fellow humans in the workplace are going to develop that level of connection and commitment. As the organization evolves and matures, as strategic priorities shift, and as we grow, some of our fellow humans just aren't going to connect and commit, and it would be unreasonable to expect them to do so, especially if dramatic shifts happen in the organization (mergers, acquisitions, and the like are infamous for this). Instead of engaging, the right choice for some of our fellow humans will be exiting so that they can pursue work that is better aligned with their own missions and goals. We owe our fellow humans the autonomy to make their own decisions to engage or exit in pursuit of satisfaction, fulfillment, self-actualization, and flourishing.

This tends to be an uncomfortable conversation because the standard HR playbook has viewed voluntary attrition as a defect for so long, but when a parting of ways happens because an employee just isn't that into us, it's often a positive outcome for both the organization and the individual. Both engaging and exiting will occur, both outcomes are valid, and both should be valued.

Humancentric leaders are not exclusively idealistic; they don't believe that every single human should connect with and commit to the work of their organization. They have a pragmatic side, and know that our fellow humans are individual semiautonomous agents in their own lives, with their own unique needs, aspirations, fears, and motivations. None of us is a bit player in someone else's story; we're each the main character in our own.

Humancentric leaders want their fellow humans to attain fulfillment and to make the greatest contribution they can make to the world. Sometimes, that contribution will happen within our own organizations, but if it needs to happen at another organization, we support our fellow humans in making a transition with respect, honor, and integrity. It'll be a better world when everyone feels an emotional connection and commitment to whatever they consider their "work," but that can't happen in just one organization. When we try to "engage" every single employee in our single organization, we're doing it *to them*, and losing integrity.

If we want to do engagement *with* our fellow humans instead of *to* them, we have to stop engaging employees. To honor one another's complex and individual humanity and autonomy, we have to turn our attention away from trying to make our fellow humans think, feel, do, or be anything they don't authentically choose for themselves. Then, we can turn our attention toward cultivating and cocreating workplaces that our fellow humans will choose to engage with. We embrace the fact that we can't engage employees, and we turn our attention to cultivating a culture that inspires engagement.

The dreaded C word

Oh, now I've gone and done it. I've brought up the most overused and least understood word in the business lexicon: culture. And I'm sorry. But we really have to wrap our heads around this one if we're going to stop engaging employees. In fact, it's low-key what this book is actually about.

You've heard all the bromides and cliches. "Culture is the way we do things around here." "Culture is an organization's personality." "Culture is values plus behavior." "Culture is what we do when no one's looking." "Culture takes over when the CEO leaves the room." "Culture eats strategy for breakfast."

I'm not saying that any of these statements is completely inaccurate, but I will say that they're inadequate. These aphorisms don't tell us anything about how to cultivate an awesome workplace culture that inspires engagement. The standard definitions and cliches turn culture into an intangible, amorphous monster that we can't control and that constrains what's possible. This mystification of workplace culture makes it difficult to understand, much less change. After all, if culture is the inexplicable and ineffable "way we do things around here," what on earth can we do to improve? If we want to do that, we're gonna need something stronger.

First, we need to understand that all of those things that get labeled as "culture"—from how people dress to what kind of snacks are in the breakroom—aren't really culture. How quickly people reply to Slack messages or how much risk the product team takes definitely characterize what it *feels like* to work in a place. But they aren't culture; they're the artifacts and outcomes of culture.

My definition of culture is heavily influenced by Human Synergistics, an organizational development research, and consulting firm. It's also influenced by Edgar Schein, who's probably the smartest living thinker about such things. And it's probably influenced by a gazillion other smart people, so credit where it's due. But here's what it comes down to.

Culture is what we think is expected of us.

That's it. And all that other stuff—like whether your boss wishes you a happy birthday or whether Linda from purchasing yells at you for borrowing her stapler—is a *result* of culture (well, Linda might have some other stuff going on too).

Barring a handful of sociopaths, most of us will behave based on what we think is expected of us. If we believe we're expected to avoid rocking the boat, we'll hold our tongues instead of pointing out how inefficient that assembly process is. If we believe we're expected to motivate our fellow humans with friendliness, we probably won't yell at them (well, Linda might; poor Linda).

OK, so if culture is all about what we believe is expected of us, where the heck do those beliefs come from? They don't come from the posters on the wall. They don't come from the employee handbook. They don't even come from what the boss explicitly *tells you* is expected. We get these ideas about what's expected of us over time as we learn and experience things together in the workplace.

Let's say I work in the telephone customer service center of a large corporation, with posters all around me that say things like, "Customers first!" and "We are here to serve!" I might initially believe that I'm expected to put customers at the center of my decision-making and daily work.

But then I have my first quality-coaching conversation with my supervisor. First, she walks me through the quality checklist, pointing out the times when I failed to greet the customer in the prescribed manner and when I failed to ask the required "have-I-completely-resolved-your-issue" question at the end of several calls. Then, she walks me through my performance metrics and explains that my average handle time—the time I spend talking to a customer and resolving their issue—is higher than the target of three minutes and 39 seconds. She shows me how all the members of my work team rank, with me at the bottom. She provides some helpful coaching on how I can better "control" customer conversations and get customers off the phone more quickly.

Each time I meet with my supervisor for a "one-on-one," our conversations follow this template. She praises me for my progress on compliance with the checklist and on my decreasing call handling time, and points out the areas on the checklist or on my metrics where I can improve. If we talk about customers or service at all, it's parenthetical.

Over time, I develop some beliefs about what's really expected of me, and they have much more to do with these conversations with my supervisor than they do with those posters on the walls. I come to believe that I'm expected to comply with rules and get my customers off the phone quickly. My coworkers likely believe the same. And our supervisor believes she's expected to enforce compliance and efficiency, based on what's she's learned and experienced during her tenure.

And as time goes on, our customer service center develops a culture of compliance and efficiency instead of service. Senior management wonders why the posters aren't working and customer satisfaction scores keep going down.

Eventually, some leader will get fed up and decide that some kind of intervention is needed to "fix" the culture—a series of training classes, an inspirational speech, more posters, more metrics, more rules. This leader will recruit others to design and build a better culture. You've probably seen this before. How successful do you think they'll be?

Are you a carpenter or a gardener?

That last bit points to a very common and completely mis-guided assumption about how culture works—that it can be designed and built. Borrowing terminology from General Stanley McChrystal's book *Team of Teams* and Alison Gopnik's book *The Gardener and the Carpenter,* we'll call this the carpenter mindset to summarize the belief that all we need is the right plans, the right raw materials, and the right tools to build a truly great culture that cultivates engaged employees.

A culture carpenter believes that they start with a vision of an ideal culture. They then design a foundation, usually with some cleverly worded aspirational values—that is, some things they *wish* were true about their organization, but aren't really happening today. On this foundation, the carpenter will probably build some policies and processes that they expect to bring those values to life. Finally, they'll add some management structures and rules to bribe and berate employees to adopt and comply with the values, policies, and processes.

The culture carpenter mindset is grounded in 19th century, mechanistic understandings of human motivations, needs, and behavior. In simpler and more stable times, maybe—maybe—this made sense. Back then, humans weren't viewed as much more than a "means of production."

But things are different now. We live in a VUCA world (that's volatile, uncertain, complex, and ambiguous), but it's also a world in which value is created through human interactions, and in which culture has an enormous impact on other business results. To continue to view humans as if we're nothing more than extensions of machines is not only insulting, but limits what's possible and is downright destructive.

So instead of trying to be carpenters, successful leaders—and when I say leaders I simply mean humans who are committed to bringing out the best in their fellow humans—take the approach of gardeners. Culture gardeners know that their fellow humans are unique, semi-autonomous plants that *want* to thrive, bloom, bear fruit, and flourish, so they cultivate the conditions in which flowers bloom, vegetables grow, and all kinds of beautiful plants gradually crowd out the weeds. But gardeners don't "build" gardens, and they don't control all the outcomes of their gardens. They can't say, "I want 12 cucumbers over there and 17 sunflowers over there."

Gardens don't work that way because—like our workplaces and our world—they are volatile, uncertain, complex, ambiguous, and emergent places in which countless factors come together to influence the outcomes. And many of those factors—rainfall, sunshine, pests, disease—are outside the gardener's control.

So instead of trying to *design* and *control* the garden, the gardener collaborates with nature, practicing a few key disciplines consistently over time, to *cultivate* the conditions in which it's more likely that their cucumbers and sunflowers will thrive. And the gardener pays attention, sensing and responding to change, repeating those key disciplines, such as planting, feeding, watering, and weeding.

The successful leader's role is to be a culture gardener, cultivating engaged employees—not creating them. The truth of this analogy can be found in the etymology of the word "culture," which was first used in the middle of the 15th century, when it meant, "the tilling of land" or "the act of preparing the earth for crops." It comes from the Latin verb *colere,* which meant to till or cultivate. Look it up!

The six disciplines of cultivating humancentric workplaces

When we take the approach of being culture gardeners instead of culture carpenters, we can start to cultivate workplaces that aren't just "customercentric" or "employeecentric", but *human*centric.

A humancentric workplace puts humans at its center. It's that simple. It's a workplace that values humans, regardless of whether those humans are labeled "employees," "customers," "suppliers," or even "shareholders," and for that reason, it's built to meet the physical, emotional, social, and psychological needs of humans. Humancentric workplaces enable humans to make awesome contributions and become the best versions of themselves, and these workplaces contribute to a more just, equitable, and inclusive world.

To cultivate humancentric workplaces, we need to commit to just six key disciplines. To make them easy to remember, I've begun them all with the same letter. The 6 Es of humancentric workplaces are the culture gardener's equivalent of planting, feeding, watering, and weeding:

- **Empathize.** In a humancentric workplace, humans listen to each other to develop empathy. The first E, Empathize, is all about listening deeply. It's learning our soil, our weather, our indigenous plants, and everything else that will influence the health of our garden.

- **Encourage.** The second E, Encourage, is all about involvement. In a humancentric workplace, humans fully participate in creating their own communities and contexts. We're preparing the soil, figuring out our irrigation needs, and reading our seed packets to figure out where the plants will thrive.

- **Educate.** In a humancentric workplace, we co-create a shared understanding about what's important, why we're here, and how we can help. We amend and till the soil.

- **Enable.** We hold ourselves to high standards in a humancentric workplace, but with the fourth E, Enable, we also make sure that we have the knowledge, tools, resources, and skills we need to achieve those standards and make our greatest contributions. We fertilize and water our garden.

- **Empower.** In humancentric workplaces, we make it easy for our fellow humans to do the right thing and contribute their unique genius to the problems and opportunities we face. With the fifth E, Empower, we review policies and processes that get in the way, and we implement new policies and processes to grease the skids. We weed the garden and get rid of barriers to thriving.

- **Embrace.** To reinforce expectations and our carefully cultivated shared understanding, the sixth E, Embrace, reminds us to recognize and reward the attitudes, mindsets, behaviors, and outcomes we expect of ourselves. We're primping and pruning our plants so that they keep thriving.

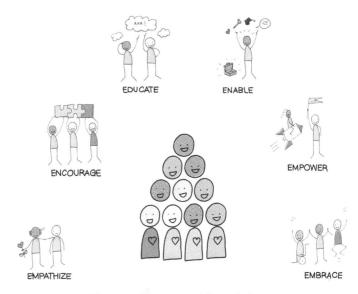

The 6 Es of humancentric workplaces
Illustration by Chantel Botha

The foundation of the 6 Es—the context of our garden—are a few key elements:

- **Vision.** What's the world we want to help create and be part of? What contribution will we make to that world? Why is that important?
- **Mission.** Why do we exist today? What's our passion and our purpose? If we were in a completely different industry, would our reason for existence be different, or would it be the same?
- **Strategy.** How do we plan to approach the fulfillment of our mission and attainment of our vision? How will we organize? Where will we focus? Why?

- **Goals.** In the near-ish term, what do we need to accomplish to advance our strategy? What organizational outcomes do we need to see, and by when?
- **Behaviors.** What behaviors do we need to exhibit to achieve our goals, execute our strategy, fulfill our mission, and attain our vision?
- **Mindsets.** What thoughts, beliefs, and assumptions do we need to develop to support the behaviors we need, the goals we'll accomplish, the strategy we'll execute, the mission we'll fulfill, and the vision we'll attain?
- **Attitudes.** How do we need to feel about our work and our fellow humans so that we can meet our goals, fulfill our mission, and attain our vision?

In the following chapters, we'll go into detail on each of the disciplines of the 6 Es. For now, though, consider asking yourself these questions to solidify what we've talked about so far:

1. What terms that I use in my daily work-related conversations and thoughts might have the inadvertent effect of dehumanizing or limiting my fellow humans? Common examples include: human resources, human capital, employee, customer, upskilling, and reskilling. What other examples can I think of? Why do these words matter?

2. What are some of the implications for me personally if I stop engaging employees like a carpenter and start behaving more like a gardener? What limitations does

this definition impose on me and my organization?
What possibilities does this shift create?

3. What is the most important priority in my organization
   right now? What does our organization need to accomplish? Who does our organization need to become?
   Why is that important now?

4. What mindsets, attitudes, and behaviors do I and my
   fellow humans in the workplace need to adopt in order
   to achieve the above? Be as specific as possible.

5. What would have to change for my organization to shift
   its focus from products and profits to human needs,
   aspirations, fears, and motivations? How possible does
   that kind of shift seem?

INTERLUDE: ABOUT ATTITUDES, MINDSETS, BEHAVIORS, AND OUTCOMES

Throughout this book, I'll use these four words a whole bunch:

- Attitudes
- Mindsets
- Behaviors
- Outcomes

These are the four pillars of individual human effectiveness in the workplace. In a way, they're like the fruits, flowers, and vegetables of our culture garden, and they are what enable the organization to achieve what it most needs to achieve and to become what it most needs to become. As such, it's probably worth a few minutes to define these terms and to understand their distinct identities. If you're as much of a nerd about this stuff as I am, you might recognize something here similar to business theorist Chris Argyris's ladder of inference, and I proudly claim that as an influence.

Attitudes

For the purposes of this book, attitudes are a largely emotional concept. They represent how we *feel* about certain things. For example, in the workplace, I might feel like I need to look out for myself, or I might feel like I belong to something bigger. I might feel safe and loved, or I might feel threatened. I might feel helpless or helpful.

Attitudes are related to, but somewhat distinct from, beliefs. Beliefs, especially about what's expected of me in the workplace, are formed over time as I learn and experience things, and begin to notice patterns. They begin to move from the realm of feeling into the realm of thoughts and, as such, are more closely related to mindsets.

Mindsets

Again, other definitions exist in the world, but for the purposes of this book, mindsets are a largely intellectual concept. They represent how we *think* about certain things. For example, I might think that purpose is more important than profit. I might think that people are less important than rules in the workplace. I might think doing things right is more important than doing them quickly. I might think it's better to do what I'm told than to rock the boat. I might think taking care of customers is less important than taking care of the company.

Mindsets and attitudes are interrelated. How I think about things can influence how I feel about them, and vice versa. A feeling of being threatened, for example, might cause me to think that other people can't be trusted, or thinking people can't be trusted can lead to a feeling of being threatened. Let's not try to impose too much linearity on complex stuff like this.

Behaviors

Ok, maybe it isn't necessary to define behaviors, but rather than assume it's self-evident, I'll feel better if we establish an operational definition that we can come back to throughout this book.

Behaviors are actions that we and our fellow humans take and, in this context, particularly actions that we take habitually. A one-time action, such as bursting into song in the workplace because I'm overcome with happiness, is not, for our purposes, a behavior. However, my habit of greeting everyone I meet in the workplace with a song might be a behavior. More helpfully, behaviors that matter in the workplace include showing up early (or late) for meetings, saying hello to fellow humans in the hallways, reviewing my work to make sure it's of the highest quality, etc.

Behaviors are the only element of the four that can be explicitly coached in the workplace. It's difficult to know what a person's attitude or mindset is, and anyone who labels someone else's attitude or mindset is usually making an assumption, based on behaviors. For example, you might assume that I think being on time doesn't matter because you've seen me show up late many times. Or you might assume that I feel confident because I always speak up in meetings. And your assumptions would be wrong.

Here's another layer of complexity. While it's true that attitudes and mindsets are often the parents of behavior, it's also possible for behaviors over time to change attitudes and mindsets. For example, I might think that employees who speak up in the workplace often suffer consequences. But if my compassionate boss encourages me to start speaking up more and, over time, I find that my speaking up is received well, praised, and even rewarded, my mindset is likely to change.

Our experiences in the workplace over time create our beliefs about what's expected and valued.

Behaviors have tremendous developmental value in the workplace, both because they can, when managed carefully, lead to changes in attitudes and mindsets, and also because they can—much more easily than attitudes or mindsets—be objectively observed, identified, and tracked in the workplace. You can't be sure that I think being on time doesn't matter, but you can be absolutely sure whether I show up to a meeting on time. For this reason, as we begin to develop a vision for the future of our organization, we should focus on observable behaviors, while being mindful and respectful of the attitudes and mindsets beneath them.

Outcomes

Another word whose meaning might be self-evident, but that will still benefit from a clear definition in this context. Outcomes are the results of behaviors over time, and for our purposes, refer specifically to business-relevant results. For this reason, outcomes are often the things that show up on an organization's dashboards and/or key performance indicators.

Outcomes, at the highest level, are likely financials, like revenue, cost of goods sold, profitability, etc. They might also be results that drive those financials, such as customer satisfaction, productivity, and yes, even employee engagement. Of course, the outcomes that matter most—like self-actualization and flourishing—are the hardest to measure.

I think that takes care of the flowers, fruits, and vegetables. Now, on with the show!

~ 3 ~

EMPATHIZE

Illustration by Chantel Botha

<u>In a humancentric workplace, humans listen to each other to increase mutual understanding.</u>

*"Most people do not listen with the intent to under-
stand; they listen with the intent to reply."*
STEPHEN COVEY THE 7 HABITS OF HIGHLY
EFFECTIVE PEOPLE

When I think back on that conversation I had with the telco executive all those years ago, it's not his words that bug me, or his lack of emotion—or even the fact that he still had a little bit of alfredo sauce in the corner of his mouth.

No, I think the reason that interaction has stuck with me for so long is that he demonstrated absolutely no curiosity. Didn't he want to know why I was asking this impertinent question? Given the same situation, I'm guessing most employees in that particular organization would've either sucked up or complained to him. Why was I asking questions about the reasons for the company's existence? What did I *really* want to know? What difference might that knowledge make in my connection and commitment to my work?

He didn't care. Wasn't interested. It didn't seem to occur to him to wonder about me.

And I don't blame him for that. As far as he was concerned, I was irrelevant. What did I have to do with the dozens of big decisions he needed to make that day? Not much.

OK, maybe I do blame him a little bit. I blame him for his lack of curiosity, which is perhaps the greatest weakness any of us can have as leaders. Without curiosity, we can't have empathy. And a leader without empathy is like a gardener without soil (we'll leave hydroponics out of the metaphor for now, k?).

If we want our fellow humans in the workplace to feel emotionally connected and committed, we'll have to develop empathy. And if we want empathy, we'll need to start listening. The first step in cultivating a healthy garden is to understand the soil, the climate, and the plants.

As we discussed earlier, the traditional approach isn't to listen, but to tell. But do we really believe we can *tell* our way to an authentic emotional connection and commitment? Unfortunately, most organizations (and most of us as leaders) haven't put much effort into developing listening muscles, and the listening we do is frequently shallow and ravaged by an epidemic that swept through organizations over the last century: efficiency. And the truth is, good listening doesn't always look "efficient."

One of the most popular investments organizations are making in employee engagement is surveys—lots and lots of surveys. Whether they're paying to participate in a benchmark like Great Place to Work (or one of many similar offerings), administering their own homegrown surveys, or buying one of a gazillion "employee engagement" software platforms, companies have clearly gotten the message that they need to survey their employees. In recent years, more vendors have popped up with twists on the survey, trying to provide more real-time measures of employee attitudes and sentiments. Still other vendors are providing tools that help organizations turn actual behavioral, operational data into conclusions about employee engagement.

On one hand, this is good news for all of us. It wasn't all that long ago that the idea of trying to understand how employees felt or thought about their employer was ludicrous. "Why would we do that? Employees should do what they're told and be grateful for the paycheck they receive in return. Their satisfaction, fulfillment, self-actualization, and flourishing are none of my business." The fact that organizations have implemented formal methods for listening to their employees is a good thing, for the most part.

Unfortunately, for many organizations, "employee engagement" and "employee survey" have become synonymous. On more than one occasion, a leader has invited me into a discussion about "employee engagement" that turned out to be about survey development, with no thought to what might be done with all the information and insights the survey might yield.

And it's not just surveys; it's town halls, one-on-ones, skip-levels, and any number of other tactics that organizations implement ostensibly to listen to their employees. Listening is a critical first step, but if our attempts to "engage employees" start and stop there, the effect is more likely to be negative than it is to be neutral or positive.

To understand why listening alone isn't improving employee engagement, try this little experiment. Ask your significant other or someone close to you how their day was, and assure them that you want to hear all about it. Listen closely as they tell you about their day. When they pause, ask a follow-up question, like "And then what happened?" or "How did you feel about that?" Keep asking questions and listening, but don't provide any feedback. Turn off your social skills and avoid saying empathetic things like "That must've been frustrating" or "It sounds like you're upset." Once you've heard it all, walk out of the room without a word and don't bring it up ever again.

OK, please don't do that to anyone you love. It's too cruel. I hope I'm not too late.

But I hope you take my point. In organizations, it's worse, in some ways, because the employee spends a significant amount of time and effort—and even takes some personal and professional risks—to provide feedback to the employer, and then the employer is the one who walks out of the room without a word.

Most organizations I speak with tell me that they've seen response rates on their employee surveys decline steadily. Some have even implemented incentives to shore up declining interest. But is it any wonder that employees have stopped responding when they see nothing being done with their feedback and the time they've invested?

Organizations—many with the best of intentions—are hurting employee engagement by making employees feel "listened to" but not heard. They're using any number of listening tactics that they've read about in Harvard Business Review or in some well-written LinkedIn article, but they're not learning from that listening, taking action, or closing the loop with employees to let them know what happened to the feedback they gave. And without all of that, can you really call it listening?

The sad truth is that listening has taken a backseat to score-keeping. Organizations can easily roll out a survey, derive from that survey some kind of score they call "employee engagement" or "employee satisfaction" or "employee experience," and then they either celebrate or lament the difference between this year's score and last year's. That's not listening. We have become too dependent on surveys as listening tools, and we've transformed them into scoreboards. Not coincidentally, as we drift further from humancentricity, the same thing has happened with listening to customers. We focus too much on the scores, and not enough on the lessons (and literal words) behind them.

While surveys can be a quick and easy way to gather information, their resolution is rather low; that is, the information gathered from surveys is often not detailed, not actionable, and raises at least as many questions as it answers. No high-resolution substitute exists for real conversations and interactions between fellow humans. After all, as I noted before, human interactions *create* value.

Our goal with this first discipline, Empathize, is to develop two kinds of empathy for our fellow humans: cognitive and affective. Cognitive empathy means, "I understand your experience." Affective empathy means, "I feel your experience." In the end, we should be able to understand and feel the answers to two basic questions:

- What do each of my fellow humans need to be successful?
- What's getting in their way?

To be clear, a leader's job is *not* to solve all of their fellow humans' problems; it's to help those humans become the best versions of themselves. For now, though, it's enough to simply develop empathy through the answers to those questions. And to get to those answers, we have to start listening.

ALARMS: A better form of listening

While Empathize is about listening, it goes deeper than what passes for listening in organizations today. In Empathize, we listen deeply to our fellow humans so that we can understand their needs, aspirations, fears, and motivations. The goal of this kind of listening isn't to derive a score or to understand the "average" employee's experience, but to connect, one human to another, developing both cognitive and affective empathy.

The inspiration for Empathize comes from human-centered design (HCD), aka design thinking. In HCD, the assumption is that one can't design a product or experience for a user without deeply understanding their needs. Product designers, for example, use ethnographic research techniques to understand who users are, how they use things, and how a given product fits into their lives. They use this approach to design products that solve real problems and meet real needs.

In the context of the 6 Es, listening can and should take myriad forms. One-on-one conversations, focus groups, and informal discussions are just some of the methods we can use to develop empathy for our fellow humans in the workplace. Assessments like StrengthsFinder, DISC, Enneagram, and Working Genius can also be valuable tools for listening to, and developing empathy for, your colleagues. A combination of approaches is likely to be far more effective than any one method will be.

But the foundation of it all, the listening tool that simply can't be replaced, is the good ol' conversation. In our conversations and interactions with our fellow humans, we can make our listening effective by following what I call the ALARMS method:

- **A:** Ask the right questions
- **L:** Listen carefully to the responses
- **A:** Ask followup questions
- **R:** Reflect what you heard
- **M:** Mull over what you heard later to identify patterns, problems, and opportunities
- **S:** Summarize and close the loop

Before we go on, I'll acknowledge that an acronym like ALARMS can be a little, well, alarming, while listening to others should be anything but. I hope that the unfortunate title doesn't distract you from the value of the framework, but instead, only serves to help you remember it. Now onward.

The first four steps in the ALARMS listening approach—ask, listen, ask, reflect—happen while you're engaged in dialogue with your fellow humans, while the last two steps—mull and summarize—happen afterward, and often follow multiple conversations with multiple people. Don't worry if this doesn't totally make sense just yet. It'll become clear as we dig into the elements of the model in just a minute.

THE ALARMS LISTENING FRAMEWORK

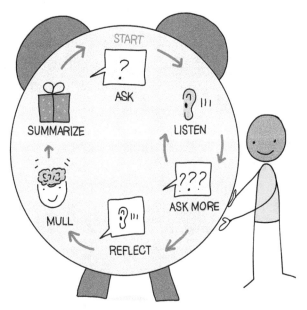

illustration by Chantel Botha

It might help to think of a real-world example. Have you ever watched a really good interviewer? In his Netflix show *My Next Guest,* David Letterman offers, in my opinion, a shining example of actively listening to understand. In his early career, Letterman focused on being funny and having laughs with (and sometimes at the expense of) his guests. However, in his current incarnation, the veteran host seems more interested in connection than comedy. He asks questions intended to reveal the real person beneath the celebrity personae of his guests, listens intently to their responses, asks incisive follow-up questions to clarify and deepen his understanding of them, and reflects back his understanding to give them the opportunity to agree or to correct any misapprehensions. Very occasionally, Letterman will relay a brief observation or story from his personal experience, but he only does this to strengthen the connection and rapport, and he's always careful not to speak more than his guests. If you or someone you know has a Netflix account, I highly recommend checking out an episode or two of Letterman's show to learn from a master listener.

Ask the right questions

Though listening might sound like a passive and reactive activity, all of the 6 Es require us to take action, and Empathize is no different. While our fellow humans in the workplace might voluntarily share an insight here or there, many organizations have developed norms that inadvertently discourage candid feedback and asking for help, so we'll have to use our positions of leadership, whether formal or informal, to get the conversation started. A leader, after all, is anyone working to bring out the best in their fellow humans. That's us.

Let's start with asking the right questions. Unfortunately, "how's it going?" and other similar questions rarely yield insights that lead to cognitive or affective empathy. If our goal is to deeply understand our fellow humans, we'll want to consider questions like these:

- What do you think is the most important thing for our organization to focus on right now?
- Why do you think that's important?
- How does that affect our employees, customers, shareholders, suppliers, and community (aka humans)?
- What do you think your role is in supporting that priority?
- What do you need to be successful in supporting that priority?
- What gets in your way or makes it difficult for you to support that priority?
- What are you most excited about?
- What are you most concerned about?
- How can I help?

These aren't the only questions; no doubt you can come up with some that are better. The point is to ask questions that are open-ended, that leave plenty of room for our fellow humans to explore what's important to them. Closed-ended questions (yes/no, multiple-choice, true/false) rarely lead to powerful insights. Best to avoid leading questions too, which start with phrases like, "Don't you think..." or "Wouldn't it be better if..." Those are statements, dressed up like questions.

Spend some time planning what you want to ask. In this kind of listening, we don't even have to know what we're going to do with the answers. Just plan questions that get a conversation started, and know that we'll be asking follow-up questions that we can't even plan for.

Listen carefully to the responses

Our next job is to listen actively and carefully. This might sound rudimentary, but the truth is that we're rarely called upon to listen well, so our muscles can easily atrophy. Don't be ashamed if you need some tips and practice to do it well.

Careful listening, with the intent to understand, starts with emptying all preconceptions out of our brains. It's only natural for our internal monologue to be louder than the voices outside of our heads. Our brains have evolved to be very good at observing what's going on around them, making judgments, and defending themselves, but if we want to listen to understand someone else, we'll have to turn off the judgments, turn off the defenses, and silence the internal monologue. This is, of course, easier said than done, but thinking that we already know what we're going to hear is one of the most-persistent barriers to listening, so it's imperative. Here are just a few tips to help us focus on the other person's words instead of our own internal monologues:

- **Drink plenty of water.** This might seem like it has nothing to do with listening, but when we're dehydrated, our ability to think clearly is compromised. According to a 2018 study by Matthew Wittbrodt and Melinda Millard-Stafford, people who have lost just 2% of their body mass in fluid have impaired attention and decision-making skills, both of which are pretty important to careful listening. Sorry if that's a little—ahem—dry.

- **Get plenty of sleep.** Again, this might appear irrelevant, but sleep deprivation also impacts our cognitive ability. In fact, a study back in 2000 by Dr. A.M. Williamson and Anne-Marie Feyer found that going 17-19 hours without sleep (i.e., getting 5-7 hours of sleep) resulted in response times on cognitive tests that were equivalent to—and sometimes worse than—a blood alcohol content of 0.05%, which is like having two drinks. Perhaps that research was enough to lull you to sleep, but I'm guessing you wouldn't slam a couple shots before sitting down to talk with a coworker.

- **Don't interrupt.** While it might not be our intent, when we interrupt, we send the message that we're impatient to get to the point, which can have the effect of shutting down open dialogue. Plus, we often interrupt when we assume we know what someone's going to say, which leads us to the next point.

• **Discard assumptions.** Assumptions act as filters that cause us to hear what we want or expect to hear, instead of what's actually being said. To the extent possible, try to shut down the part of your brain that's evaluating and turn up the part that's fully present.

• **Take notes.** While we don't want to get preoccupied with our written words in a way that takes our attention away from the person we're listening to, taking notes can be useful to keep us present and to help us remember what we're hearing. And as old-fashioned as this sounds, consider taking notes with paper and pen instead of an electronic device. Our phones and computers are filled with distractions, and even if you're paying close attention, it can appear otherwise when you tapping away on your phone. I like to use special notebooks that are made for scanning later so that I can easily turn my analog notes into digital.

• **Focus on feeling as much as meaning.** It's important for us to understand the meaning of what our conversational partners are saying, but it's equally important to understand the feeling as well. Since we're ultimately looking for an emotional connection and commitment, feelings will play a vital role as we move forward with the other Es. Was that a shudder in their voice? A sigh? Did they get louder or quieter? If you're listening closely, you can hear feelings.

- **Watch for nonverbal cues.** Words are important, but our faces and bodies can say a lot without uttering a syllable. Keep an eye out for open and closed body language, for facial expressions, and fidgets. We often gloss right over these because it's not "polite" to look at folks that closely, but when we tune into the non-verbal, we'll gain further information and insights to make what we hear even more meaningful. And, just in case it's not obvious, this is as important for on-screen conversations as it is for in-person ones—maybe even more so. We've been on Zoom long enough by now that we all should be better at noticing all those visual cues.

Ask follow-up questions to clarify and deepen your understanding

While I look to David Letterman as an example of a great interviewer, I more often see truly terrible interviewers in my real life. Their exchanges often look like this:

- Interviewer: [asks a good question]
- Interviewee: [gives a thoughtful and honest response]
- Interviewer: [nods and asks next question on the list]

This is not good listening. A good listener knows how to ask follow-up questions that reveal more details and in-sights, clarify the interviewee's main points, and deepen the understanding and rapport between them. Of course, we'll wait until our conversational partner pauses before we ask. Because good follow-up questions are asked in response to what you've heard, it's impossible to plan them. However, below are a few examples of generic follow-up questions or the beginnings of more specific ones:

- Tell me more about that.
- How does that feel?
- What do you think that means?
- What did you take away from that experience?
- Why is that important to you?
- What about that is most important to you?
- Help me understand...
- Can you explain...

Of course, follow-up questions aren't just a technique; they should be asked to elicit more information and add to the value of what we've already heard. As our fellow human is responding to our follow-up question(s), we'll need to lean in and listen again with the intent to understand.

Reflect what you heard

The biggest mistake we can make as listeners is assuming that what we heard is what our fellow human actually meant. Reflecting back what we heard is a necessary step to ensure shared understanding. The purpose is to let the person to whom we're listening know what we've come to understand, based on what they've said, and then give them the opportunity to agree or clarify.

If you've ever taken a class or watched a video about empathic (or active) listening, you've probably heard reflection statements. They often begin with "What I hear you saying is," "It sounds like you're saying," or something like that. Notice that they don't start with "You're saying." The critical element of a reflection statement is that it reflects *your understanding* of what was said; it isn't a reflection of what was meant. Positioning our reflections as being about *our* understanding will open up the opportunity for further clarification and will minimize defensiveness.

So let's say the fellow human we're speaking with says, "There's a small in-group of employees at this company who make all the decisions."

We can unpack a lot from this statement. To start, we would, of course, ask some follow-up questions. I would probably say, "Tell me more about that," to get the conversation started, and I might ask, "What bothers you most about that?" to dig a little deeper into the truth. Once the person was finished, I'd reflect by saying, "It sounds like you're feeling left out of decision-making, and maybe like it's unclear to you how decisions get made in this company. Is that right?"

Our job of reflection isn't over until the person to whom we're listening says, "Yes, that's right." If they say anything other than yes or its synonyms, it's time to ask more clarifying questions. "Kind of" or "basically" don't count; you're looking for unambiguous assent.

Mull over what you heard later to identify patterns, problems, and opportunities

Empathizing doesn't end when the conversation is over. If we've had a lot of great conversations with our fellow humans about what's going on in our workplace, what's important, what's exciting to them, what concerns them, what they need, and what gets in their way, then we're probably sitting on a ton of information that hasn't turned into empathy just yet.

To make all of that information useful, we'll need to sit with it, swim around in it, admire it, and digest it. Our goal shouldn't be to reduce all of the complex individuals with whom we spoke to a monolithic oversimplification. Instead, our goal is to appreciate the heterogeneity of experiences, the multiplicity of perspectives, and the spectrum of needs, aspirations, fears, and motivations that our fellow humans carry with them. You're a gardener, sifting the dirt through your fingers, noticing whether there are minerals, worms, rhizomes, or mycelia. Is the dirt hard and bright like clay, or soft and dark like coffee?

This can be a little overwhelming—especially when there are things we don't want to hear.

Our brains naturally prefer to simplify the complex, to turn observations into facts, and basically to make things as easy as possible. But if you've been human for any amount of time, you probably already know that we are beautifully and frustratingly complicated, unique, unpredictable, and individual, and the job of a humancentric leader is to appreciate and honor that.

To make this job a little easier, though, here are some questions we can ask ourselves as we roll around in all the information we gathered from conversations with our fellow humans in the workplace:

- What did I hear most often?
- What jumped out at me? Why? (The "why" is important here because things can jump out because they're important, but they can also jump out because of our own predispositions, prejudices, and assumptions.)
- What surprised me or was unexpected?
- What were the most extreme perspectives I heard?
- What contradictions did I hear?
- What general conclusions might I draw from all this information?
- What evidence exists in the information that my general conclusions are wrong?
- What concrete actions could I or others take to make sure that most of my fellow humans had what they needed to succeed in the workplace and in their lives?
- What barriers to success and fulfillment could I or others remove?

Notice that these questions won't lead us to any simple conclusions or pithy statements to put on a PowerPoint slide. However, they'll help us fully appreciate the perspectives of our fellow humans, and to move closer to cognitive and affective empathy.

Summarize and close the loop

The last phase in the ALARMS framework is also the most difficult. After we've been soaking in all this information for so long, we'll begin to feel comfortable with its complexities and contradictions, but we'll also need to take two important steps:

1. Communicate what we've learned with others
2. Let all the folks with whom we had conversations know what we learned and what we plan to do about it.

For the first step, the hardest part of the job will be resisting the temptation and external pressures to oversimplify. It's likely that our peers will want to hear statements like, "Employees feel like this," or, "People are saying that." These statements will be lies. Avoid them. We owe it to all the people who gave us their candid perspectives to continue to honor their individuality, their idiosyncrasies, and their weirdness. They trusted us; don't make them regret it by turning them into averages or stereotypes.

The good news is that we will have done the hard work in the "mull" phase. As we communicate with others, we'll reveal the complexities and contradictions, the surprises and the so-whats, and let them experience the same joy and confusion that we did as we swam around in that information.

The one place where we can save folks a little time is in our review of the answers to the last two "mull" questions. These will become our recommendations. What concrete actions can we and our fellow humancentric leaders (again, formal or informal) take to make our fellow humans in the workplace more successful and fulfilled? What knowledge, skills, tools, or resources can we provide? What barriers can we remove?

Know that these recommendations aren't going to meet the needs, allay the fears, stoke the motivations, or fulfill the aspirations of every human in our workplace, but make bold bets on steps you can take to help the most people. That's all any of us can do.

For the second step, the job is pretty simple, but no less critical. If we want to cultivate a humancentric workplace in which our fellow humans believe they are expected to share their perspectives candidly and clearly, then we must let them know that we heard them, that we understood them, and that we're committed to doing something in response. We can use more or less the same framework as we used to communicate with others, but when we get to those recommendations, we'll share only those that we have some certainty will happen. We don't have to be 100% sure, and we can communicate any dependencies as we share with our fellow humans, but we'll make sure they know that something concrete will happen as a result of the time they invested. For bonus points (and a preview of the next chapter), we can invite the folks from whom we learned so much to participate actively in designing and implementing solutions to problems or approaches to opportunities. More on that when we get to the second E.

Keep listening

The listening process described above is, in a way, an event. It's an event that should occur frequently, but it's a targeted effort to develop a sound foundation of empathy. However, it isn't the only way, and it isn't sufficient to develop empathy across your organization. To make sure that happens, we'll need other listening posts. Some of these will be always-open —like a Denny's or the passenger-side window in a 1997 Toyota Corolla—and others will be periodic. The most important of these is the one-on-one meeting.

Regular one-on-ones

When done well, one of the most powerful listening tools in any organization is the one-on-one meeting. This is a regularly occurring conversation between a manager or supervisor and the humans for whom they're directly responsible. If they're not happening in your organization, get them started. If they are happening, make sure they're being done well.

Over the years, I've worked with many organizations who tell me that one-on-ones are common, but on closer examination, I find a few pitfalls that make these one-on-ones less effective:

- They're irregular and/or infrequent.
- They're one-way status updates.
- They're task-centric instead of humancentric.
- They're optional.
- They're casual.

From the above list, you can deduce what I believe to be the keys to effective one-on-ones, but let's dive into the details.

- **Effective one-on-ones are regular and frequent.** Regularity means that they happen on a predictable timeline. They shouldn't just pop up ad hoc or whenever it occurs to us to schedule them. Both parties should have reasonable certainty about when they'll happen. Frequency is a bit more subjective and context-dependent. Monthly one-on-ones might feel frequent to you, but, as your employee, I might feel like too much time elapses and too much changes from month to month for that to be effective. As a rule, the lower person in the hierarchy should determine the frequency, assuming you're in a hierarchical workplace like most of us. This enables the person with less power to make sure their needs are being met, and that the meetings aren't based on the convenience of the person with more power. When we truly Empathize, we redistribute power and increase symmetry within hierarchical relationships.

- **Effective one-on-ones are dialogues.** They accomplish something that an email or a project management tool can't. Don't waste this valuable interaction time exchanging status updates about various work projects; tools exist to meet that need effectively, efficiently, and asynchronously. Have a real human conversation that creates value. Whether you're the supervisor or the employee, use the questions from the first A of ALARMS as a guide to get the conversation going:
    - What do you think is the most important thing for our organization to focus on right now?
    - Why do you think that's important?
    - How does that affect our employees, customers, shareholders, suppliers, and community?
    - What do you think your role is in supporting that priority?
    - What do you need to be successful in supporting that priority?
    - What gets in your way or makes it difficult for you to support that priority?
    - What are you most excited about?
    - What are you most concerned about?
    - How can I help?

Make the one-on-one a dynamic exchange that creates value for both parties by sharing with each other.

- **Effective one-on-ones are humancentric, not task-centric.** Depending on the expectations that have existed before now, it can be easier to default to task-centric conversation. "What are you doing about this?" "How's that going?" These conversations aren't bad, but they leave a lot of value on the table, especially if we're committed to truly empathizing with our fellow humans. Get personal. Disclose elements of your life that create connection, trust, and rapport, and encourage the same. If you're asked how you're doing, answer truthfully. Talk about the good and the bad. Offer support. Help each other. Treat each other with dignity, respect, and admiration. Get uncomfortable. The connections we create through real interactions create new possibilities.

  ○ At some point, we'll have to grapple with our own vulnerability. That's become a trendy word, and things that are trendy should always be regarded with a smidgeon of skepticism. But Empathize is based in trust, and that trust is based in vulnerability. A funny thing about trust is that we usually have to extend it to others before we start to get it, and before our fellow humans have "earned" it. Otherwise, we won't get anywhere.

  ○ At the same time, we will respect our fellow humans' boundaries. Just because we're eager to "go deep," get vulnerable, and be "radically candid," it doesn't mean that all our fellow humans are ready for it. Begin where your relationship is right now, and work toward greater intimacy and vulnerability as you sense readiness and willingness. Don't be a creep.

- **Effective one-on-ones are not optional.** Of course, situations will arise in which they need to be skipped or rescheduled, but as much as possible, behave as if that isn't an option. Reschedule with that customer. And that meeting you were invited to, but you can't figure out why? Decline it. Make room for the one-on-one.

- **Effective one-on-ones are disciplined.** I don't mean they need to be formal (nor should they be put in time-out), but they should receive the same level of attention and preparation as any other use of your valuable time. Both parties should come prepared, should be 100% focused on the conversation, and should take notes. What do you want to be different after this one-on-one? Work toward that, and don't waste each other's time.

Other listening posts

Conversations that occur between humans are required for anyone who wants to cultivate a humancentric workplace, but other methods for listening can complement our conversations. In fact, it's helpful to have a variety of "listening posts" available so that our fellow humans begin to believe that speaking up and listening are expected and valued.

Following are some ideas for additional listening posts to implement in your humancentric workplace, but feel free to add your own ideas too:

- **Skip-level meetings.** With a similar structure and rigor as one-on-ones, a human has a dialogue with their boss's boss.
- **Suggestion box.** Much maligned, but only because of poor use and management, when done well, this always-open method (which can be online or IRL) lets your fellow humans in the workplace know that you're always listening.
- **Town hall meetings.** Not to be confused with all-hands meetings or similar mechanisms for delivering information, the humans in the lower ranks of the hierarchy should do most of the talking in these dynamic, slide-less exchanges of ideas and perspectives.
- **Interdepartmental meetings.** These can take many forms, including demo days, presentations, or open discussions, but the goal is to increase awareness of interdependency and broaden empathy across the organizational silos.
- **Surveys.** Done poorly, surveys are a poor substitute, but done well, they can provide useful high-level information to feed into further listening efforts, while also acting as an indicator of overall humancentricity. To do surveys well, make them part of a comprehensive listening strategy that gathers quantitative and qualitative data; don't let a survey be your only listening post.

- **Pulse surveys.** Short, targeted, and frequent, these surveys are great for checking in on one specific element of your fellow humans' experience in the workplace. Just make sure that your organization is prepared to quickly understand and take action on the feedback.
- **Externally moderated focus groups.** While there's no substitute for building and cultivating connections among the humans within your workplace, it's sometimes beneficial, depending on your organization's history, to bring in a disinterested professional to conduct some of the initial listening sessions.

One listening post that's wildly popular but rarely effective is the open-door policy. "Come on in! My door's always open," says Boss. There are a few common ways in which this approach tends to fail. The first is that those with open doors are just way too busy. The only reason the door is open is because they just left (*rimshot*). They're almost always in meetings, almost never in their offices, almost never available for a quick online or in-person chat, and when they are, they're desperately trying to meet a deadline. So they're available, but not really.

The second failure mode for open-door policies is that those lower in the hierarchy are afraid to take advantage of them. If your organization doesn't have a history of inviting and acting on candid feedback, or worse, if your organization has a history of treating candid feedback with disregard or disdain, there's no reason to expect folks to suddenly walk through the open door.

The third failure mode for open-door policies is that they become ways to pass monkeys from one person's back to another. If you're concerned that I've lapsed into absurdist prose, I highly recommend checking out the Harvard Business Review classic, "Who's Got the Monkey."

Simultaneously dated and timeless, this brilliant essay by management experts William Oncken, Jr., and Donald L. Wass dissects a very common organizational dysfunction in which people managers take on all their employees' problems. The article was originally published in 1974, so it's filled with dehumanizing terms and concepts, but it's also filled with important insights about what it means to manage and lead.

If you take on the problems of all the humans for whom you're most directly responsible, you're not likely to be able to address them all, and you're also likely to drop the ball on other responsibilities that might be more important or impactful. As Oncken and Wass teach us, effective managers and leaders collaborate with those for whom they're responsible to better understand their problems, develop approaches or solutions, and implement them, all while letting those with the problems continue to own them and their solutions. This not only preserves your limited personal resources, but also develops and supports the contributions that others can make (more about that in Encourage).

Empathy in action

OK, Eryc, you say, these seem like good ideas, but how do I actually do it? How can I begin to cultivate empathy and better listening throughout my organization?

Many years ago, I worked in a large customer service department in a business-to-business company, where I was responsible for employee communications and engagement. One day, a batch of customer survey results came in, and the news was not good. Customers, many of whom were large businesses themselves, did *not* like doing business with us. They found our billing practices difficult, cumbersome, and opaque.

Management's response to these survey results was predictable: they called a meeting and yelled at the customer service employees, demanding that they do better. Management's assumption, I suppose, was that the low survey scores resulted from their fellow humans being *unwilling* to do what was necessary to meet their customers' needs. A good berating from the boss always leads to better customer service, right?

As this bullshit rolled downhill, it landed in my boss's lap, who promptly delivered it to me. "I want you to travel to all of our customer service centers and deliver training on customer service skills," he said. His assumption, I suppose, was that the low survey scores resulted from employees being *unable* to do what was necessary. I agreed to do it, but first, I asked if I could convene a facilitated workshop with management to get clear on their vision of a successful outcome. Thank goodness he trusted me and was willing to make that happen.

In this workshop, I encouraged management—from the vice president to line supervisors—to envision a future in which customers loved doing business with us. In that envisioned future, I asked them to tell me what observable behaviors they saw more of or less of when compared with the current state. This only took about 45 minutes, at the end of which, we had a list of behaviors that would be necessary to improve customer satisfaction. I promised I would incorporate this into my next steps.

What I did next wouldn't look like customer service training to most people, and I don't suppose it was. Because I had worked side-by-side with many of the customer service agents for a long time, I had a slight advantage over management in diagnosing the root cause of the problem. While management assumed agents were unwilling, and my boss assumed they were unable, the truth was neither. Agents weren't lacking in motivation or skills. They didn't need training. They needed help. They needed to be listened to, empathized with, and supported. My assumption, I suppose, was that the low survey scores resulted from a lack of emotional connection and commitment, not knowledge and skills.

Instead of delivering a boilerplate how-to training course, I traveled to each of our company's customer service centers and conducted listening sessions with the customer service agents. In these sessions, I asked questions much like those listed earlier in this chapter:

- What does good customer service mean to you? What does it look like?
- Why do you think good customer service is important to our company right now?
- To provide excellent customer service as you've defined it, what tools, skills, or resources do you need that you don't currently have?
- What gets in the way of providing excellent customer service, as you've defined it?
- What else do you need to be successful in your role?

During these sessions, I listened carefully, took pages of notes, and asked dozens of follow-up questions. And I committed to summarizing their feedback and bringing specific recommendations back to management.

After these sessions, my fellow humans, some of whom I was meeting for the first time, wanted to take me out to lunch, dinner, and drinks. They wanted to continue the conversation. Many of them told me they'd worked at the company for years and had never participated in a workshop like that. Some said they'd never been asked questions like that by their supervisors or managers. In other words, they'd never really been listened to. Management had frequently come to them with demands and requests, but rarely with questions. A sincere "how can I help?" is sometimes all it takes.

Empathy never ends

While tactics and specific processes can be followed to develop empathy in your organization, the overarching process of empathizing is cyclical and never ends. In fact, it might be helpful to think about the ALARMS framework for listening and developing empathy as ALARMSALARM-SALARMSALARMSALARMS ad infinitum. If you're committed to developing a humancentric workplace, you'll follow the cycle around and around, and you'll encourage your fellow humans in the workplace to do the same.

The 6 Es framework for authentic employee engagement and cultivating a humancentric workplace is built on the foundation of listening and empathy. Without that solid foundation, the rest of the framework is likely to crumble. To ensure your foundation is sound, please re-read this chapter before you move on to the next. After you've read this chapter at least twice, answer these questions:

1. Am I ready to take on a full-fledged listening exercise, or do I need to take specific actions to prepare for the kind of deep listening that Empathize suggests?

2. Am I the right person in my organization to do this listening, or should I work with and coach someone else?

3. What can I do to encourage more listening and empathy within my organization? What are the barriers?

4. What small change can I make tomorrow to begin cultivating greater empathy with my fellow humans in the workplace?

~ 4 ~

INTERLUDE: ABOUT "WORK" AND "JOBS"

Throughout this book, I refer to "work," and it's entirely possible that you've reasonably interpreted that as a synonym for "jobs." But for the purposes of this book, the two words and the concepts they represent are starkly differentiated, so let's get into it.

Let's start with what those two words have in common. They're both four-letter words, so that's fun, but not particularly significant. They both refer to labor, which is often that activity we do so that we can wear clothes, eat food, and live in shelters of some kind. But that's about it.

For the purposes of this book, a "job" is that thing you do to earn money. You might have chosen it, and you might not've. You might find it satisfying and fulfilling, or you might loathe it. Either way, your relationship with your "job" is likely instrumentarian in nature; i.e., you see your job as a means to an end, not as an end in itself.

We can change jobs all the time. Most folks have many jobs throughout their lifetimes. We can find jobs, and we can lose jobs. Our jobs can be taken over by artificial intelligence or other machines.

My dad, who passed away recently, had many jobs in his lifetime. He was a veterinary assistant, a short-order cook, a marine biologist, a geologist, a spectroscopic chemist, a pet-store owner, a dog obedience trainer, and a high-school chemistry teacher. Those were his jobs.

But his work was the throughline that connected all those things. My dad's work was helping people and animals. Whether he was analyzing water for safety, helping folks care for their animal companions, or teaching unenthusiastic teenagers the laws of physics by lying on a bed of nails (something he actually did in his high-school classroom), my dad was working to improve life for humans and animals, even though he might never have articulated it in just that way.

If a job is that thing you do to "earn a living" (a terribly problematic phrase that should be reconsidered; do our fellow humans have to "earn" the right to be alive?), then your work is that thing you're doing throughout your life, and of which you might not even be conscious.

And while your work might be ambitious and grandiose, it might also be practical and close-to-home. Maybe your work is streamlining processes and making them less effortful. Your work might be keeping things clean. Or looking out for those closest to you. Or creating art.

Your work is satisfying and fulfilling, in and of itself. You might get a little jolt of happiness with the completion of a given task or with helping a specific person, but that's not the sole reason you do your work.

Your work is also never done. There might come a time when you're no longer able to do your work, but there won't come a time when your work is done.

You can quit your job, but you can't quit your work. A machine can take your job, but it can't take your work.

When I say that work is one of the ways in which we seek satisfaction, fulfillment, self-actualization, and flourishing, I'm not talking about your job. I'm talking about your work.

If a job is a human *doing*, then work is a human *being*.

I'm a huge rap and hip-hop fan. Years ago, clarifying the difference between those two related concepts, the pioneering rapper and educator KRS-One said, "Rap is something you do. Hip-hop is something you live."

When it comes to jobs and work, a similar rule applies. A *job* is something you do. Your *work* is something you live.

~ 5 ~

ENCOURAGE

Illustration by Chantel Botha

<u>In a humancentric workplace, humans fully partici-pate in creating their own communities and contexts.</u>

"...every healthy individual must labour enough for his food, and his intellectual faculties must be exercised not in order to obtain a living or amass a fortune but only in the service of mankind."
MAHATMA GANDHI ASHRAM OBSERVANCES IN
ACTION

On an almost-weekly basis, some kind and well-intentioned manager asks me some version of, "How do we get our employees to...?" It might be, "How do we get our employees excited about our mission?" Or it might be, "How do we get employees to be more productive while they're working from home?"

But the idea that we can make our fellow humans do things—an idea at the heart of traditional change management—is antithetical to a humancentric workplace.

Now, before you get the wrong idea, I'm not throwing shade at the profession of change management. The discipline has evolved over time and probably contains the initial seeds of a humancentric approach to the workplace. In its inception, the acknowledgment that individual humans are the units of organizational change was revolutionary.

Change management is one of the longest-lived and respected disciplines of organization development. I have long been a practitioner and an evangelist of Prosci's human-centered methods and tools for increasing employee adoption, usage, and proficiency. If you're not familiar, Prosci is a global leader in researching, codifying, and disseminating effective change management practices, and their ADKAR methodology (which stands for Awareness, Desire, Knowledge, Ability, and Reinforcement—the five preconditions they've identified for human behavior change) has been an enormous influence on the ideas in this book. Of course, there are myriad other schools of change management out there, but

I'd argue that no one has done more to advance and productively complicate the discipline of change management than has Prosci.

But, in my experience, while it is possible to change our fellow humans' behaviors, especially in the short term, that's merely an exercise in cultivating conformity and compliance. It's about people doing what they're told and/or what everyone else is doing. If you take an Industrial-Age approach to work, that might be all you need. Conformity and compliance are the chocolate and peanut butter of old-school management.

They're also the world of the carpenter. The carpenter needs their lumber to conform to certain measurements—lengths, widths, shapes, angles—and then they need to follow a plan to the letter to build a cabinet, a table, a building that looks just like the plan.

As I'm sure you've already discerned, I'm not here for that. You can get certain results in your workplace through conformity and compliance, but you can get even better results through emotional connection and commitment, the kind that leads to changes in attitudes and mindsets, as well as behaviors—the kind that leads to human satisfaction, fulfillment, self-actualization, and flourishing.

It's easy to argue that managers only need to worry about the behaviors, but leaders like you already know—even if you've only had fleeting glimpses—how much more productive our fellow humans are when they're connected and committed to their work than when they're simply doing what they're told. They might even achieve positive outcomes we couldn't envision or anticipate.

You can spend the precious minutes, hours, and days of your life trying to get people to change their behaviors, and a lot of folks do. It's the equivalent of turning your multidimensional garden plot of infinite possibilities into one rectangle full of soybeans, instead of collaborating with nature to see what wants to grow and thrive. This approach is completely understandable. After all, it's much more difficult to change attitudes and mindsets. However, it's also much more valuable if you're trying to cultivate a humancentric workplace.

There are implications for this (as there are for most of the ideas in this book) beyond the workplace. What we experience at work crosses and spills over into other areas and other people in our lives.

Putting aside other humans for now, what kind of world do you personally want to live in? Do you want a world in which you do as you're told and what everyone else is doing? Or would you prefer a world in which you do what you do because you're deeply connected and committed to it? The former is the world of traditional management. The latter is a world of authentic engagement and liberation. It's the world that can exist when we stop "engaging" employees and start creating the conditions in which our fellow humans *choose* to engage, in which they're so emotionally connected and committed to their work that they willingly and pro-actively go above and beyond to help the organization attain its vision, fulfill its mission, and achieve its goals, while be-coming the best versions of themselves.

Just like you, when your fellow humans feel heard and un-derstood (through Empathize), they'll have a greater desire to get involved with the strategic priorities and visions. In-volvement and participation are at the core of the second E, Encourage.

Before we go on, I just want to acknowledge that the work you've chosen to take on—of relinquishing illusions of control over your fellow humans, of embracing your role in helping them make meaningful contributions and self-actualize—is really freaken difficult. The much easier path—like much, much easier—is to pretend that the way we've always done things is the right way. The job of the average manager in a modern organization is really hard, and the job of a humancentric leader is even harder. So even as I challenge you through this book in ways that demand more of you, I also encourage you to take care of yourself, be kind to yourself, and give yourself room to screw up every once in a while. You're of no use to anyone if you're all used up. If you feel yourself getting overwhelmed, give yourself a break. Take a nap. Rub a dog. Grab an iced coffee. Go for a walk. Hug someone you love. Or just notice that overwhelm for a second and thank it. And know that it'll get easier.

In the spirit of that, within the second E is a gift that I'd like to give to you right now:

It's not your job to solve all the problems in your organization.

Let me just say that again: it's not your job to solve all the problems in your organization.

If you're a supervisor, manager, director, vice president, or in any other position beyond the bottom of the hierarchy, I know it can feel that way. It can feel like your success is judged on your ability to personally take care of everything. You identify a problem, figure out how to solve it, and then expend massive effort trying to coax and cajole all your employees to adopt and implement that solution. But how's that working out?

I'll take this gift a step further: if you decide it's your job—and yours alone—to solve all the problems, you will quickly receive lessons in people's resistance to *being changed*. Remember that people don't resist change; we resist being changed. So you're not doing yourself or your organization any favors by trying to be a one-human problem-solving machine, especially when you know that, at some point, you're going to need the cooperation and collaboration of other humans to implement your brilliant vision. And if you're trying to make a really big change, an important change, a momentous change, you'll need those fellow humans not just to change their behaviors, but also to change their attitudes and mindsets. In other words, you'll be trying to change their hearts and minds, how they feel and how they think.

When was the last time you successfully changed someone's mind? If you have been successful, you'll know that it wasn't a matter of simply convincing that person with impassioned pleas or well-reasoned arguments. Bribes and threats didn't do it. Instead, there was probably something new that the other person had to experience, a bit of alchemy that had to catalyze the ingredients, and a whole lot that was well outside of your control. In fact, if you reflect honestly, you might conclude that you didn't change that person's mind, but that they changed it themselves.

It's no different in the workplace. Organizations don't change, motivate, engage, or even satisfy employees, at least not in any meaningful and lasting sense. If employees are changed, motivated, engaged, or satisfied, it's because they have changed, motivated, engaged, or satisfied themselves (insert the giggle of a 12-year-old me here).

But you wouldn't be reading this book if you hadn't recognized a problem or an opportunity, something that you wanted to change. And if your fellow humans in the workplace aren't emotionally connected and committed to their work, that's probably the situation you want to change. Or you want it to change itself. In that way, you're hoping that your fellow humans will change their attitudes, mindsets, and behaviors, so that you can achieve even greater (quantitative) or better (qualitative) outcomes. By now, you realize that you won't change those people, but that they will change themselves, if you can cultivate the right circumstances.

Once you've listened to and empathized with your fellow humans in the workplace, it's time to start involving them in the change you wish to co-create, and that's what the second E is all about.

The case for Encourage, which is about involvement and participation, is quite simple. When the people who have to change their attitudes, mindsets, and behaviors are involved in creating the future, they'll be more likely to embrace it, and you won't have to do as much of that thing called "change management."

Tools for inviting and involving your fellow humans

One company I worked with addressed Encourage by hosting a contest called "Things That Make You Go Hmmm," an homage to the 1991 C&C Music Factory hit. I encourage you (see what I did there?) to take a quick break to dance to it. I'll wait here.

OK, welcome back. For this contest, the company invited employees to submit their ideas for the worst things that the company forced its customers to do. Employees quickly submitted dozens of ideas that I've seen crop up in multiple organizations: making customers provide the same information multiple times, making customers work with several different (and disconnected) employees to solve their problems, forcing customers to use the company's preferred communication channels instead of their own, etc.

"Things That Make You Go Hmmm" was a fun way for the leadership of the company to involve employees in a strategic vision of becoming more customercentric, and it also led to a list of things the company should *stop* doing.

In the world of organizational development, there's a very useful tool that's commonly used, called **start/stop/continue**. Once an organization has determined what it wants to accomplish, how it wants to accomplish it, and who it wants to be while accomplishing, it can use this tool to drill into tactics:

- In order to accomplish what we want, how we want, while being who we want, what will we need to *start* doing?
- In order to accomplish what we want, how we want, while being who we want, what will we need to *stop* doing?
- In order to accomplish what we want, how we want, while being who we want, what will we need to *continue* doing?

This is an extraordinarily useful tool for turning lofty, theoretical goals into actions that can be taken. Like most organization development tools, this isn't some esoteric and mind-blowing technique that requires an advanced degree, but it provides a simple, accessible framework for making the intangible a little more tangible.

When I use this in organizations, I often find that the **stop** and **continue** lists are longer than the **start** list. In other words, what's often standing between who an organization is and who an organization wants to be is extraneous activity.

For example, I do a lot of work with organizations that say they want to become more customercentric. When we use **start/stop/continue** with front-office employees who work with customers every day, they can often point to several things they're already doing that support the goal (**continue**). They'll also make a short list of new things they could try (**start**).

But their longest list is usually **stop**. Your fellow humans, especially those who work directly with your customers, have intimate and vivid knowledge of all the things you do to your customers (or to each other) that you should stop doing.

Another useful tool that is similar to **start/stop/continue**, but even simpler and more explicitly focused on behaviors, is **more of/less of**. I mentioned using this tool in the Empathize chapter. With this tool and a clear vision of who we want to be and what we want to accomplish, we and our fellow humans can brainstorm specific, observable behaviors that we'll need to see **more** of or **less** of in the envisioned future.

The key to this exercise is to focus on *observable* behaviors. Often when I use this with organizations, participants will offer up ideas like wanting to see more "can-do attitudes" or less "siloed thinking." These are examples of attitudes and mindsets that we want to change, and those are important, but they're harder to confirm and always subject to interpretation. To keep this brainstorming on track, I encourage participants to focus on behaviors they could see or hear, listing only things they could capture with a video camera.

To make the **more of/less of** exercise even more valuable, it's helpful to make sure the parallel lists aren't just the opposites of each other. It's easy for groups to get into the mode of listing things like, "more working together" and "less people working alone at their desks," but these parallels aren't that helpful. Encourage the group to highlight behaviors they've actually seen that they want less of. As with **start/stop/continue**, you're likely to end up with a longer "less of" list. For example, organizations that are becoming more humancentric often express that they want to see **less of** "leaders telling people how to do their jobs," "whispered conversations in the hallways," or "meetings that could've been emails."

Encourage in action

By now, it's probably clear what "encourage" means in the context of the 6 Es, but I find it's always helpful to learn from real-world examples.

A few years ago, a large provider of internet and television services in South Africa realized it had a problem. It was the incumbent in its territory, the proverbial giant in the market-place, but something was happening. All over the area, small competitors were popping up and eating into the company's market share by being more nimble, more flexible, and more focused on their customers. When the company realized this, it decided that it needed to become more customercentric.

Now I think we already know how I feel about that term, but put that on hold for a moment, because this ends up being a story about a very humancentric approach to a business problem.

Before we get to what this company—we'll call them Acme because I loved Road Runner cartoons when I was a kid—did to become more customercentric, let's talk about how most companies would tackle this problem.

Thinking back a few pages in this book, you'll probably re-member the three traditional methods of leading change in organizations: **broadcast**, **bribe**, and **berate**. Plenty of orga-nizations I've worked for and with over the decades would have taken the following approach:

- Convene a group of senior leaders to create a well-worded statement about the organization's focus on customers (precursor to **broadcast**)
- Conduct a "road show" in which executives share the statement with all employees and tell them how

important it is and how much everyone needs to change (**broadcast** and **berate**)

- Create a one-way communication campaign to further broadcast the well-worded statement (**broadcast**)
- Create some kind of bonus program that gives employees extra money when they achieve "customer-related" goals (**bribe**)
- Require all employees to attend "training" that tells them about the well-worded statement, why it's important, and what they need to do to support it (**broadcast** and **berate**)

Technically speaking, this approach follows several change management "best practices," but it dehumanizes our fellow humans in the workplace, treating them as "targets" of various interventions, and it sets out to "engage" them as if they *aren't* semiautonomous agents within a complex adaptive system. Don't be alarmed if this approach seems very familiar (and even "right") to you; there's still hope.

Acme went about things completely different. See if you can spot elements of the second E, Encourage, in their approach:

- Convened a group of senior leaders to review complaints, employee feedback, and other data related to their customers' experience of doing business with the company
- Based on this review of data, created a list of the company's top 100 customer-related problems

- Assigned the top five problems to members of the executive team, who addressed these problems personally, while an internal communications team captured them on video to share with the whole organization (conveying the level of commitment the C-suite had to the effort)
- Invited employees to submit their solutions to the remaining 95 problems
- Directly involved employees in implementing their proposed solutions

If you review that approach again, you'll find few signs of broadcasts, bribes, or berating. Acme approached their goal like a gardener instead of a carpenter. This is because Acme had three assumptions going into this effort:

1. Employees, not management, would have the best ideas because they worked most closely with customers.
2. Employees didn't need to be "trained" in how to be "customercentric" because they already had the necessary expertise.
3. Involving as many people as possible throughout the company would lead to the best solutions.

While Acme's story presents a clear example of Encourage in action, it's important to examine the results it achieved as well. First, more than a third of the company's workforce submitted suggestions for improvement, an excellent indicator of their emotional connection and commitment to the work that needed to be done. And second, within 12 months, the company had addressed all 100 of its customer-related problems. Rather than creating an elaborate marketing campaign about their customer-centricity, they simply acted in customercentric (and humancentric) ways. As my writing teachers used to say: show, don't tell.

Pitfalls in Encourage

When I speak to leaders in organizations about **Encourage**, the two most common objections I hear are: (1) we don't have time to involve everyone in everything, and (2) we can't include everyone's opinion on every decision. I agree completely—or mostly. Since these objections are related, let's tackle them together.

Since I promised not to bullshit you, I'll say it plainly: Involving everyone equally in everything will be cumbersome, time-consuming, and a general pain in the ass, and I wouldn't recommend it. Prioritization is the key here.

To wrap our brains around this, let's adapt an idea from one of the smartest people I know, Tim Creasey, Chief Innovation Officer at Prosci. In evaluating a strategic change or initiative, we'll determine the benefits we expect will accrue from that change, and then what percentage of the benefits are dependent upon our fellow humans connecting with and committing to the change. If the percentage is relatively low, perhaps we can just decide on a course of action, announce it to our fellow humans, and move on. For example, if we've decided to start using pink sticky notes instead of blue sticky notes, we can simply remove pink sticky notes from the office and stock up on blue ones. The benefits we're expecting to get (whatever those might be in this terrible example) aren't dependent on our fellow humans at all. We don't need to involve everyone in solving every problem, implementing every solution, or making every decision.

But if the percentage of benefits dependent on the emotional connection and commitment of our fellow humans is high, then involvement and participation are likely to get better results than simply deciding and announcing. For example, if we've decided to shorten all meetings from 60 minutes to 50 minutes, we can use technology to help us, but we're still going to need some connection and commitment to the why, what, and how of this from our fellow humans, so involving them is likely to help.

Oh, but involving our fellow humans can really slow things down, can't it? It's so painful to get everyone to participate and join an effort, isn't it? Can't we just skip to the end and then worry about bringing our fellow humans along after we've solved the problem?

We absolutely *can* skip right past Encourage. We can choose not to invite our fellow humans to participate in addressing our most critical strategic priorities, and instead just tell them what to do. However, at that point, we'll probably have a whole lot of change management work to do—broadcasting, bribing, berating, coaxing, cajoling, and convincing. We'll be back to trying to get our fellow humans to do things.

And that's going to slow us down too, while it takes us off the path to humancentricity.

When we have ambitious and glorious visions of a better future, the likelihood of our attaining those visions and their attendant benefits is directly related to the level of connection and commitment that our fellow humans feel to them. We'll need their help to overcome the status quo, to get to that bright future, and to sustain the new ways of working, doing, being, and thinking. The work of cultivating that connection and commitment can happen along the way, or it can happen at the end. Either way, we'll need to do that work.

But here's the thing. If we do the work of Encourage by involving others along the way, the odds that we'll end up with better outcomes are extremely high. Diversity of perspectives, thoughts, inputs, and approaches leads to better solutions, so there's a double benefit to involvement and participation.

In addition, the work of after-the-fact change management to achieve the same level of connection and commitment is expensive, exhausting, and often less effective. Who wants to do that, when we can just make our lives easier—and our workplaces better--by involving our fellow humans up front?

Use Encourage wisely

Remember that not every decision or every organizational initiative is right for involvement and participation. As we've already noted, most organizations won't function effectively with 100% democratic decision-making. In fact, relying on participation in everything can actually prevent an organization from attaining its vision, fulfilling its mission, and achieving its goals. Encourage is a strategic approach, not a tactical one, so use it when cultivating connection and commitment with your most important priorities.

Empathize + Encourage = healthy soil for the humancentric garden

While they're just two of the 6 Es, Empathize and Encourage represent nearly half the work of cultivating authentic emotional connection and commitment. When we deeply understand our fellow humans—upon whom our organization's success depends and whom we're here to help—and when we gain their participation in building solutions to problems and approaches to opportunities, we power up our efforts with serious juice.

These two Es also provide us with key inputs for the other Es. In fact, we won't be able to practice the other four Es effectively if we don't nail these, so this won't be the last time we talk about Empathize or Encourage.

For now, before you move on to the next chapter, I encourage you (Oops! Just like Britney, I did it again!) to spend a few minutes contemplating your honest answers to the following questions.

1. What examples from my own life can I point to in which involvement and participation of others (or of myself) made a difference, either because of their presence or their absence?

2. If I feel resistant to involving others in my most important priorities, why is that?

3. What limitations (experience, expertise, creativity, skills, etc.) might I have that could be helped by involving others?

~ 6 ~

INTERLUDE: ABOUT
GENERATIONS IN THE
WORKPLACE

Another question I'm frequently asked by kind and well-intentioned managers and leaders is how they should adapt their workplaces, leadership styles, expectations, and musical tastes for the many different generations of humans collaborating in today's workplace.

"Is it true," they ask, "that Gen Alpha won't even participate in a meeting if you don't ask their pronouns?"

It's not. But that doesn't mean you shouldn't find out their pronouns as part of Empathize.

"Is it true," they ask, "that Millennials all expect to be CEOs by the time they're 45?"

It's not. But that doesn't mean you shouldn't find out what each of the Millennials in your workplace wants, needs, hopes for, and fears. (BTW: the oldest of the so-called Millennials are already in their 40s, so...)

Here's the thing: Plenty of well-respected sociologists and researchers can derive valuable and meaningful insights from looking into generational differences. And the labels are a handy, efficient way of referring to a group of people who were born at around the same time, or who are around the same age or stage of life now.

And sometimes shortcuts (what psychologists like to call heuristics) like generational differences can help us quickly orient to changing circumstances or make low-stakes decisions.

But most—like almost all—generalizations about generational differences (easy for me to say!) are about as accurate as predicting the future based on the patterns that the last of my Smart Bran cereal makes as it floats in a puddle of oat milk.

That is to say, not accurate at all.

I mean no disrespect to diviners of the future, by the way. Many cultures all over the world have rich and meaningful histories with such practices.

But I mean to say that so-called "generational science" is not at all a science. And plenty of well-respected sociologists and researchers are discarding generational labels in their work as I type this.

In 2021, Philip Cohen, a sociologist at the University of Maryland at College Park, published an open letter in the *Washington Post*, requesting that the esteemed Pew Research Center stop using labels like Gen Z and Baby Boomers in their reporting, and calling the concept arbitrary and counter-productive. His open letter was signed by 170 other social-science leaders, so he isn't exactly alone in his thinking.

Personally, I have two primary objections to the use of gener-ations as a way of "understanding" people in the workplace —or in the world. The first is moral/ethical, and the second is practical.

I know that shortcuts are sometimes useful, but we just need to know when we're using them and be very careful about how much truth we put into them. I've seen so-called experts stand in front of crowds to explain how "this generation is like this" or "that generation really values that." Dutifully taking notes, the audience nods along knowingly, having all of their suspicions and biases confirmed. You've probably been in one of those rooms.

Now imagine if that speaker was up there making the same claims about any other demographic category. What if they were expounding on the "traits" of people from Burkina Faso? Or of people with hazel eyes? Or of people of—ahem—short stature? Making generalizations about certain races, ethnicities, ages, disabilities, gender identities, sexualities, nationalities, body types, or anything—especially any part of their being over which the person has no control—is not ok, and it's a short step from there to policies and practices that covertly or overtly discriminate against folks for those aspects of their identity. We wouldn't tolerate generalizations based on race or ethnicity, and we shouldn't tolerate them based on when folks were born either.

So that's the moral/ethical objection.

The practical objection is that these generalizations are generally pretty useless. Think about it this way. What has more influence on the person you are today: your upbringing or when you were born? Do you have more in common with folks who were born within the same 10-20 years as you, or with those who also grew up as the only kid of color in a small town?

What's more, there are so many confounding variables that make these generalizations murky, at best. We can say, for example, that Gen Z cares about purpose above all else at work, but we can't separate their stage of life (younger, fewer responsibilities, perhaps more flexible lifestyles) from their so-called generation. Similarly, we can say that Baby Boomers are stuck in their ways, but we're likely propagating destructive, ageist myths more than we're describing something intrinsic to everyone born between 1946 and 1964 (that range, by the way, is a whole adult human of 18 years old).

Sure, I'm firmly in the generation labeled X (that label, by the way, was first applied to folks growing up immediately after World War II, was later used as the name for Billy Idol's first band, and then was popularized as the tongue-in-cheek title of novelist/artist Douglas Coupland's first novel), born as I was in 1971. As such, I have some common frames of reference and experience with other folks who grew up in the United States at the same time.

However, I'm also a White, cis-gender, non-disabled, straight male. I grew up in rural Colorado with two White parents who were married and a sister. If you, too, were born within the accepted Gen X years of late '60s to early '80s, we might both remember some of the same music, some of the same world and national events, and some of the same popular culture. But if you grew up in Bangalore, it's likely we don't have much of that in common. And if you grew up also in the US, but as a Black trans girl who uses a wheelchair and was raised a single dad, our similarities are likely pretty superficial.

The point is this: generational generalizations might be useful, but they are no substitute for actual social science. They are no substitute for getting to know your fellow humans. And they're no substitute for real, meaningful empathy and connection. For that reason, you won't see or hear me mention them again in this book, except possibly as a shortcut to refer to folks who are of a certain age right now. So we'll leave that concept behind.

~ 7 ~

EDUCATE

Illustration by Chantel Botha

In a humancentric workplace, we educate and become educated to create a shared understanding about what's important, why we're here, and how we can help.

"People need to be reminded more often than they need to be instructed."

—SAMUEL JOHNSON

Have you ever attended a training class at work, and left completely unchanged? If you're like most people in the corporate world, the answer is yes. For example, every year, your company requires you to complete some kind of online course about harassment and discrimination in the workplace. You can click through the modules, answer the quiz questions, and complete the training, but if I ask you the next month—or even the next day—how to handle a specific situation involving harassment or discrimination, you're unlikely to be able to recall and apply any of the contents of the course. In other words, you went to "training," but you didn't learn. And that's not your fault.

Remember that time when I was told to deliver "customer-service training" to a bunch of experienced professionals who didn't need it? In that moment, management believed that they (and I) knew things that our fellow humans didn't about customer service, and that we just needed to "train" them. That is, we needed to transfer what we knew to them. This is what we often mean when we use the word "educate" in a corporate context. Simple, right?

Before we get into what the third E is all about, I want to make it perfectly clear that it is *not* about training. Over my years of using the 6 Es with organizations, this has been one of the most common misconceptions, and it's totally my fault, so let's just clear it up right now.

When leaders tell me they have a problem and that they think the solution is training, my years in organization development (which included a stint of managing training for a multi-billion dollar company) give me the confidence to tell them they're wrong—most of the time. That might sound a bit arrogant, but let me explain.

Training is an activity; it is not an outcome. When a leader says their employees need training, what they really mean is that their employees need to know or be able to do something. In other words, what the organization needs is learning, which *is* an outcome. It's the process of obtaining, evaluating, and synthesizing new information (knowledge or skills) in a way that can be applied.

Most corporate training is dull, ineffective, and does nothing to help an organization attain its vision, fulfill its mission, and achieve its goals. And it does even *less* to help the organization's people attain more satisfaction, fulfillment, self-actualization, or flourishing. In fact, most corporate training is (like the harassment and discrimination example) a compliance exercise, with little to no return on the investment. This is no one's fault, but it's built into a faulty system.

One of the reasons that corporate training persists, even when it doesn't add much business value, is because it is easy to measure. If you ask a manager of a business what percentage of employees have attended some kind of training, they can easily answer that question, assuming they have some kind of system for tracking such things (and they almost always do).

However, if you ask that same person what percentage of employees know or can do a specific thing, they will have a much harder time answering that question. When I managed training and development, the organization relied on me for two metrics: (1) how many people attended a given training course, and (2) how many hours each employee spent in training. Both of these metrics were all but meaningless when it came to the actual value of the learning that occurred (or didn't).

The public education system in the United States deals with the same challenge: it's easy to prove that a given student attended and passed a given course, but it's much harder to prove that that student learned anything. But we keep focusing on what's easy to measure because we can't figure out how to effectively measure what really matters.

So the next time you think you have a training problem, I ask you to consider the possibility that what you actually have is a learning problem. Training might be one way to address your learning problem, but it's probably not the only way, and it's not even likely to be the best way.

When you think about the most important things you know or are able to do, reflect on whether you attained the knowledge or skills from a class or from another more complex and sophisticated mode of learning. How did you learn to speak your native language? Or how to be a good romantic partner? Or how to respond when someone you care about is in pain?

(P.S. If you answered "TikTok" to any of those questions, I would like to meet you and learn more.)

So what is Educate?

The key question of Educate is: what *must* all of our fellow humans know or be able to do in order to be effective in their efforts to help the organization attain its vision, fulfill its mission, and achieve its goals? Where training often starts with content to be delivered, Educate starts with goals to be accomplished, and those goals are pared down ruthlessly to only what our fellow humans *must* know or be able to do.

If you're an educator or have ever been exposed to educational theory, you'll recognize that Educate starts with something like learning objectives. In my experience, there are only a few things that all humans in a workplace need to know:

- What is our most important priority?
- Why is it important now?
- How am I expected to support it?

That's really it. Depending on your answer to the first question, you might need to answer a few more. Other common learning objectives might include the ability to answer the following:

- Who are our customers, and who do they need us to be?

- Who are our employees, and who do they need their managers and leaders to be?
- Who are we, and who do we need to be for each other, for our suppliers, and for our community?

Now, if you're like most leaders I know, you're probably thinking, "Heck, I could answer those questions in an email and send it out to all my fellow humans in the next 15 minutes!"

Yes, you could. But don't be deceived. Remember that Educate isn't about training, but about learning. And that learning isn't merely individual, but organizational. Through Educate, we're trying to co-create the answers to these questions so that we develop a *shared understanding*. If our goal is simply to tell our fellow humans *our* answers to these questions, then you're right. But we're gardeners, not carpenters. We're trying to cultivate a humancentric organization in which our fellow humans develop a sense of connection and commitment to what we're all here to accomplish together. For that, we'll need to develop a *shared understanding* among our fellow humans regarding the answers to those three questions. An email isn't going to do it, nor will a training class, nor any other one-way attempt to "educate" our fellow humans.

As such, Educate requires a multipronged approach. Tactics for developing this level of understanding might include that email you wanted to send, and it might even include a training class or two, but it'll likely also mean some human dialogues, some experiential learning, and a good deal of reinforcement. Most of us learn through repeated exposure, repeated practice, and real-world application of ideas. It will be neither easy nor quick to achieve the level of shared understanding that Educate requires.

At the same time, just imagine what would be possible if all our fellow humans in the workplace actually shared an understanding of the answers to these three questions and how they apply to their specific roles and responsibilities within the organization. All else grows out from this shared understanding.

(Did I say "shared understanding" yet?)

In some organization development circles, they speak of the difference between diagnostic and dialogic approaches to leading change. Diagnostic change represents the typical, carpenter-style approach: spot a problem, diagnose what's causing it, fix the cause, enjoy your new set of cabinets.

Dialogic change speaks to what Educate is all about, which is a gardener's perspective of collaborating with our fellow humans to cultivate something together that none of us could've tackled alone. Dialogic change is created through dialogue, back and forth, co-creation of the strategy, tactics, and outcomes. I'm not saying we need to throw out the carpenter's approach altogether. In fact, research suggests that a balance of both diagnostic and dialogic processes leads to better outcomes. But there are plenty of books out there about the diagnostic approach and this book isn't trying to be another one of them. Educate is here to remind us of the dialogic approach.

In many senses, when it comes to employee engagement, Educate answers the question: engaged with what? Once our fellow humans know what they're being asked to engage with (that is, our most important priority), why it's important, and how (specifically) they (specifically) can help, they'll have a better sense of what, exactly, they're being asked to engage with, and they'll be able to make an informed decision for themselves about whether to engage or not. When Educate is done well, those who choose to engage will have a lodestar toward which they can direct their efforts. And because we've spent time previously listening, empathizing, and involving them, they'll be all the more receptive to and enthusiastic about this shared learning experience.

How to Educate

While I've now made the task of Educate a bit overwhelming and daunting, I have another gift for you: the most powerful learning will come from the learners themselves.

Think of it this way: If I were to tell you, right now, the meaning of life and your purpose within it, it might blow your mind, but you also wouldn't really understand it.

(I also don't know it, but I'm fairly certain it has something to do with the way popcorn and M&Ms taste together.)

At any rate, after I told you, you'd have lots of questions, and I wouldn't be able to answer most of them because they'd pertain to your specific circumstances, resources, limitations, past experiences, and beliefs. You're likely to get far more value out of discovering the meaning of life and your purpose within it for yourself.

So instead of seeing Educate as another exercise in "telling your way to transformation," we collaborate with our fellow humans to construct a shared understanding. This isn't a mere exercise or charade of empowerment; it's an embrace of the fact that each of us creates our own understanding of the truth. We don't actually know the answers to these questions for each of our fellow humans in the workplace, because we don't fully understand their specific circumstances, resources, limitations, past experiences, and beliefs. So instead of telling our fellow humans *our* answers to these questions, we encourage them to create their own answers and to discuss them in ways that lead to shared understanding.

OK, I think I've said "shared understanding" enough, but this might be the time to point out at that "shared understanding" is different from "the right answer." Educate assumes there are *lots* of "right" answers, and that we can each have our own "right answers" while also sharing an understanding.

To clarify, it might help to take this out of the conceptual realm for a second. If it's 52-degrees Fahrenheit (about 11 Celsius) outside, I might think it's warm and you might think it's cold. Neither of us is wrong, and we can both agree that it's 52-slash-11 degrees. We have a shared understanding of the temperature, while we have different answers.

Let's try another example, just to make sure I'm being clear. If you ask me what my favorite food is, I'll probably answer chocolate or pizza, (I know: so sophisticated.) but your favorites might be Sour Patch Kids or lobster thermidor. Even though I might think you're wrong, we clearly have a shared understanding of the concept of "delicious food," which might be sweet, savory, rich, crunchy, chewy, etc.

One way to begin the journey toward shared understanding in the workplace is with an interactive workshop. We bring together our fellow humans and have them work in groups of four to six to develop their own answers to the questions above. And while written and spoken words have primacy in the modern workplace, we'll encourage our fellow humans to break free of the tyranny of language and be more inclusive of neurodiversity by using other ways to express their answers as well. This might include images, music, movement, or any other methods that effectively convey meaning. While they're creating their answers, we'll invite our fellow humans to argue, joke, discuss, and debate. You might use world café, gallery walk, or any other facilitation techniques to enhance the experience and deepen the impact of this approach to Educate.

In the end, our workshop participants won't all have the same answers to the questions. Because their circumstances, resources, limitations, beliefs, and past experiences will vary, so will the specifics of their answers. Remember that the goal isn't for all of our fellow humans to be able to recite the same words from memory, in the way that some organizations make employees memorize their mission statements. That's just rote memorization that does nothing to cultivate authentic connection and commitment.

Instead, the goal is for our fellow humans to develop a deep and shared understanding regarding the answers to these questions. In the process, they'll develop deeper empathy for each other as well, a key ingredient in reducing the destructive power of silos and increasing our understanding of the interdependency that makes our workplaces (and societies) function.

The ROI of Educate

Back when I had that job of managing training for a corporation, I was frequently asked about the "ROI of training." If a given employee spent eight hours in a class, could I prove that the added value to the business was greater than the investment of that time? While I could make all sorts of things appear to be true in a spreadsheet, the honest answer was that I couldn't. There was no straight line from "number of employees who attended X class" or "number of hours Y employee spent in training" to decreased expenses, increased revenues, or any of those other much-coveted financial outcomes.

The truth is that there's little to no return on an investment in training. However, it's possible to obtain great returns on learning, which is what Educate is all about. To begin with, though, we have to determine what we want to accomplish.

After years of focusing my head and heart on aspects of business that are difficult to measure and rarely have dollar signs in front of them, I've learned to depend on the Phillips ROI model to help me think about the ROI of pretty much anything. The model is hierarchical, with complexity and value increasing as we rise through the levels.

THE PHILLIPS ROI MODEL

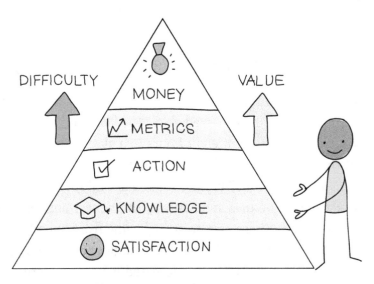

The Phillips ROI Model (c)2019 ROI Institute, Inc.
www.roiinstitute.net. All rights reserved.
illustration by Chantel Botha

Quick aside here.

We should always be a bit skeptical of models that can be easily visualized as pyramids. While hierarchical thinking is highly valued in most modern cultures, it is also often used to justify the status quo, to rationalize the oppression of the many by the few, and to maintain classist, racist, ableist, and ageist "traditions." That said, like so many mental models, pyramids can help us to better understand complex and intangible concepts by simplifying and ordering them. As statistician George Box once wrote, "All models are wrong but some are useful."

Now, where were we? Oh right: the hierarchical, pyramidal, potentially oppressive, and highly useful Phillips ROI model.

The complex and intangible concept that the Phillips ROI model sets out to visualize is that different kinds of "organizational interventions" (like the dialogic process of Educate) can have different kinds of impacts on the organization. One of the fundamental tenets lying behind the pyramid is that the "return" in "return on investment" doesn't always have to be financial. Plenty of outcomes (like human flourishing) can be positive without adding more zeroes to the bottom line.

In fact, the foundation of the Phillips ROI model, **satisfaction**, isn't financial at all. Let's say we're about to host a deep discussion with our fellow humans, but all we want is for those who attend to choose the smiley face on their evaluation forms. In this case, both the design of the event and the assessment of the return on our investment can be pretty simple. We'll design our discussion to maximize satisfaction —perhaps by providing great snacks and a facilitator who tells jokes and does magic tricks—and we'll assess our success with a question that asks folks to rate their satisfaction. Pretty easy. There might not be much learning, complexity, or financial business value here. But we all get to walk away smiling, which is some kind of return, and probably better than its opposite, right?

The next level up in the model is **knowledge**, another nonfinancial return on investment. At this level, after our deep discussion, we want our participants to know something they didn't know before. Again, the design and assessment are relatively simple. First, we determine what we want people to know. Then we assess their knowledge before and after the event. We can tell pretty clearly whether we have changed what our participants know, and a traditional training class might actually be able to accomplish this. At this level, we might say we've achieved some kind of learning with relatively little complexity, but we can't really prove any financial—or even practical—value. That said, our fellow humans know something they didn't know before, which is probably a net good.

One important thing to note here: the hierarchical nature of the Phillips ROI model implies that **knowledge** is dependent upon **satisfaction.** In other words, if we hope that folks will know something they didn't know before, we'll also need to make sure that they're satisfied. This might or might not be strictly true, but recognizing that a positive experience (i.e., satisfaction) is more likely to support learning (i.e., knowledge) is key for those of us with ambitious and glorious visions of a better future. Similarly, we'll need **satisfaction** and **knowledge** to reach the third level of the pyramid.

At this point, Educate might look like a level 2 objective in the Phillips ROI model, where people just need to know something they didn't know before, but we aim to go beyond simple knowledge to understanding, which is a form of applied knowledge. To understand is to know something *and* be able to apply it situationally. In other words, Educate is a level 3 objective.

The third level in the Phillips ROI model is **behavior** or application. Here, we're hoping that our imaginary deep discussion will change what people do. Yes, we're back to talking about behavior change. Design and assessment get a bit more complex at this level. We need to determine what behavior we want people to adopt. Then we need to figure out how best to get them to adopt it, and some way to assess whether they have adopted it or not after the fact. As we know from change management research over the decades—or from our own efforts to change our diets, quit drinking, or any number of other habits—a mere training class is unlikely to change our behavior or result in any meaningful, sustained change. No one smoking cigarettes just needs to be told that it's bad for them to make them quit. Check out Prosci's ADKAR model for more about that.

By now, you can see that level 3 of the Phillips ROI model is harder to achieve and harder to measure than the previous two levels. It's also harder to say that a given behavior changed as the result of some specific action or event (like a training class). That is, it's hard to isolate all the variables that might be influencing the outcome. If your kids suddenly start keeping their rooms clean, how certain can you be that anything you did caused it? It could've been something they picked up from a friend, from school, or from a TikTok challenge. That said, there's quite a lot of value and *potential* ROI to changing behavior or having learning applied in the workplace, assuming the behavior change is ethical (i.e., the participants are willing, and it's in their best interests).

Continuing our ascent up the Phillips ROI ladder, we get to the fourth rung, at which our deep Educate discussions have somehow affected key performance indicators or delivered some kind of meaningful **business impact**. It's self-evident, I hope, that this is not a place where training or any other single event will get us very far. Granted, some learning needs to occur to get us here, but we're well beyond the realm of level 2, when we just needed to impart knowledge. We'll definitely need some of the magic we used to cultivate behavior change, but then we'll need go beyond that to determine all of the factors within our control that will enable our fellow humans to get different results or change whichever metric we're looking at.

Making this even more complicated, to understand the true return on our investments, we'll also need to isolate the effects of our efforts from other factors that might've affected this metric. At this rung, our efforts become more complex, and our attempts to measure their effectiveness become even trickier, but we've also achieved a higher level of financial value and potential ROI.

And finally, we reach the top of the Phillips ROI pyramid. It won't surprise you to find, in the context of capitalism, that the mountaintop is **financial** impact, at which our Educate efforts have increased revenue, decreased costs, etc. You don't have to hold an MBA to know that you're not going to get here with one discussion or event. You also know that only *some* of the factors that influence financial results are within your control. You're likely to implement myriad initiatives, projects, and tactics to get to this level, and while the ROI is high, you'll have a very hard time determining which of the many Educate investments was most effective, which sort of worked, and which were a waste of time and resources.

There are also *plenty* of reasons to argue against the logic of placing financial impact at the top of the ROI pyramid, and I'd be happy to do so. For now, though, I'll simply say that I believe the most important outcomes an organization can create are human. If we broadly define the "business impact" of level 4 to include these, I'd assert that impacts on human satisfaction, fulfillment, self-actualization, and flourishing are the most valuable returns on any investment.

Educate in action

Many years ago, I was studying to become a high-school English teacher. While I didn't end up choosing that path, there's a story from that experience that illustrates what Educate (supported by Empathize and Encourage) can look like in an organization.

While I was student teaching, I was responsible for three different groups of students. One of them was much more difficult than the others. In that class, students frequently shouted, threw things, and generally engaged in behavior that made my job—and any meaningful learning—difficult. Students frequently didn't even show up. On top of that, the average grades in the class were significantly lower than my others, with many students failing.

I felt like I was failing too. I was in my late 20s and had very few tools to manage this. I tried yelling. I tried punishments. I tried speaking to a few parents. Nothing I did changed anything. I was having a terrible time, and I was pretty sure most of the students were too. My supervising teacher advised me to be tougher on the kids, to enforce harsher punishments, to send the most-disruptive students to the principal's office, but none of this felt quite right to me.

One day, at my wit's end and nearly in tears, I asked the students if they could do me a favor. I was a teacher in training, I reminded them, and still learning how to do my job. I needed their input.

It was the end of the class period. I gave each student a note-card and asked them to write on the notecard anonymously how they wanted our class to be different. They would need to give me that notecard to be able to leave the room when the bell rang. I stood at the door and waited as students passed by and dropped their cards into the box I was holding.

The next day, I transcribed nearly all of the students' responses onto large pieces of paper and posted them throughout the classroom. "Everyone is so mean to each other," said one. Another said, "I can't concentrate." Yet another said, "I wish people would listen to each other." As the students came into the classroom, I encouraged them to walk around the room and read what they'd written before making their way to their desks. It was the quietest that room had ever been.

Once everyone was seated, I facilitated a conversation, asking more questions. "What would your ideal English class look like?" "What behaviors would you like to see more of or less of in the classroom?" "What is the purpose of this class?" "What do you think your role is in making this class work?"

Some of the students were embarrassed by the truth of what they saw on the walls. Others were stunned by being asked questions instead of instead of being told what to do. All of them were attentive and engaged. The conversation that flowed was honest, vulnerable, and constructive. The students had ideas for making their experience better that I never would've thought of. They listened to each other. Even the most-disruptive students (the ones I was advised to send to the principal's office) leaned in, expressed remorse, and embraced accountability.

I'd be lying if I told you that the class was magical, tranquil, and idyllic from that point forward; it was still a challenge. One event doesn't transform a culture. But something shifted from that experience of cultivating a shared understanding. The class was quieter and more civil, and more students participated in class discussions (that's level 3 of the Phillips ROI pyramid). I also saw results that I could measure: absences went down and grades went up (that's level 4). The students had created together a shared understanding of what was important, why it was important, and what they needed to do differently, and it was more effective than anything I could've cooked up on my own and tried to get them to adopt.

I didn't know it at the time, but in this experience, Empathize, Encourage, and Educate came together to cultivate a more-constructive environment that led to better outcomes. Those students—my fellow humans in that workplace—rose to the challenge and solved their toughest problems. They didn't need to be "trained;" they needed to educate one another. And in doing so, they made their lives and mine a little better.

As activist and change-maker adrienne maree brown says, in a twist on an adage from *Tao Te Ching*, "Trust the people and they become trustworthy."

Reflect on Educate

Would you look at that? You've made it through three of the 6 Es! It probably feels like you're halfway done, gaining momentum, and just want to power through the next three Es so you can set this book aside and get to work.

While I applaud your enthusiasm and share your sense of urgency regarding humancentricity, for the sake of higher quality, better results, and a better world, I encourage you to spend a few minutes answering the following questions to help you cement your own approach to Educate:

- To what extent are my fellow humans in the workplace aligned on the answers to the three key questions (what's important, why is it important, how do I support it)?

- To what extent do *I* have answers to those key questions?

- To what extent are the senior leaders in my organization aligned on those answers?

- What have we tried previously to create a shared understanding in the organization, and how successful have those approaches been?

- What would it take for all of my fellow humans to truly understand our most important priority, why it's important now, and what their roles are with respect to that priority?

- How might I incorporate the three key questions into my Empathize and Encourage efforts?

~ 8 ~

INTERLUDE: ENGAGE YOURSELF

"I was looking for a job, and then I found a job
And heaven knows I'm miserable now."
THE SMITHS "HEAVEN KNOWS I'M MISERABLE
NOW"

The 6 Es are a valuable framework for cultivating a humancentric organization in which your fellow humans authentically choose to engage with your organization's vision, mission, and goals. They're also a crap-ton of work (if you're not familiar with the crap-ton, it's a traditional unit of measure that is roughly equivalent to a helluva lot).

But seriously, each word in this book up to this point has been like another pebble placed on your shoulders. Whether you're a senior leader in an organization or have merely assumed a position of leadership by reading this book, you've taken on an enormous responsibility. And while I applaud and honor you for taking on this daunting mission, I also want to take care of you, because we need you.

While this book is full of ideas, the work of cultivating engagement is not only the work of the mind. It is also the work of the body, heart, and soul. As such, it demands tremendous resources and resolve, and you won't come by these without planning for them. This chapter, then, is dedicated to you, to help you not only cultivate your own engagement, but also to take care of your most precious internal resources. An unhealthy gardener can't grow a healthy garden.

How self-care connects to the 6 Es

The term "self-care" gets thrown around a lot, and really gained popularity in 2020, for obvious reasons. I think it's wonderful that the concept of taking care of oneself is getting increased attention (though we should be talking simultaneously about those who do and do not have the privilege of being able to do so in our world, but that's a topic for another book), and I absolutely think that we have to take care of ourselves. However, as with most terms, I'm afraid it means different things to different people, so once again, let's take a minute to define our terms.

When I use the term "self-care," I'm referring to a structured and intentional strategy of renewing one's own resources (especially energy, but also optimism, positivity, mental health, and physical health) with the express intention of having what's needed to make your greatest contribution, to be of service to others, and to become the best version of yourself.

Notice that I am *not* referring to bubble baths, naps, or hot fudge sundaes. And I'm also not referring to the myriad "self-care products" being sold in an effort to commodify this important human need. All of those things are wonderful (man, I could go for a bubble bath right now!), and they might be tactics in a self-care strategy, but that's all they are: tactics. They also imply that self-care requires buying things. Sneaky!

Notice that my version of self-care isn't about pampering yourself; the goal of self-care is to fill your tank so that you have enough fuel to lead, cultivate, nurture, and protect others. Self-care gives you the juice you need to maintain your own sense of emotional connection and commitment to the work that lies ahead of you.

How to take care of yourself

In their monumentally awesome book *The Power of Full Engagement,* Jim Loehr and Tony Schwartz make a clear case for self-care, but they call it "engagement," which I recognize, in the context of this book, is confusing. Nevertheless, we have a lot to learn from Loehr and Schwartz. You should go read that book, as soon as you're done with this one, so I won't attempt to summarize it here. I will, however, highlight some of the book's key points that you, as a humancentric leader, should embrace with all your heart.

Loehr's career was spent coaching professional athletes and Schwartz's was in professional development in the corporate world. Together, they discovered some powerful truths that will make us all better able to serve.

The key insight, around which all others in their book revolve, is that our most precious personal resource is energy, and not time. Many of us believe that if we only had more time, we could accomplish so much more, but that belief assumes an unlimited supply of energy, which most of us don't have (and as I approach each successive birthday and can't squawk out an intelligible sentence after 8pm, I'm keenly aware of that). True, time is our most precious non-renewable resource, and we should choose how we spend it wisely, but without energy (which is, in fact, renewable), our time doesn't have much value. Thus, for maximum impact and contribution, we need to focus more on managing our energy than our time.

Loehr and Schwartz observe that we have four domains of energy to manage: **physical**, **emotional**, **mental**, and **spiritual**. As we move through our lives, we expend energy in all these areas. We spend our **physical** energy moving our bodies from one place to another (sometimes, just from the bed to the coffeemaker). We spend our **emotional** energy connecting and empathizing with others (and sometimes performing and/or managing emotions at work—I see you folks in customer service!). Our **mental** energy is expended on all the difficult thinking, problem-solving, and reasoning we have to do to get through our days. And **spiritual** energy dwindles as we strive to serve others and be stewards of our planet. And for anyone carrying around trauma, it's like a silent drain on all four domains of energy.

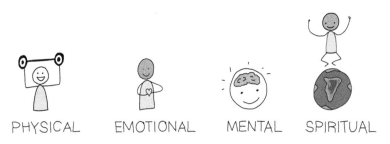

Illustration by Chantel Botha

Fortunately, there are two interrelated practices that offset this constant spending of energy and keep us from collapsing into energyless heaps. The first is rest and renewal, and the second is training. The former is exactly what it sounds like: restorative activities that enable us to replenish our energy and bounce forward with vim and vigor.

Here, it's important to note that not all rest is restorative. If my brain is feeling spent from a day of writing this book (a hypothetical situation, of course, that isn't even close to, um, well), scrolling through Instagram to look at pictures of adorable pit bull puppies might be restful, but it probably isn't going to restore my mental energy. I'll probably be better off taking a quick walk, closing my eyes for five silent minutes, or doing some focused breathing.

All right, so restorative practices can help us renew our energy, and that's pretty important and relevant to self-care, but Loehr and Schwartz's second practice to help us manage our energy is even more powerful. We can actually train ourselves to have more energy, and this is what I want you, as a gardener of humancentric workplaces, to pay attention to.

In his work with athletes, Loehr discovered the completely unsurprising fact that athletes get physically stronger as they practice. But as he looked beneath this obvious phenomenon, he found something more meaningful. The strongest and most successful world-class athletes he knew didn't just practice all the time. Instead, they alternated periods of intense stress on their bodies with periods of renewal. A muscle gets strong by being pushed to its limits, and then being given time to mend, heal, and grow. Same goes for energy.

But here's the trouble. Schwartz noticed that corporate athletes—everyday working folks like you who care about getting results and doing meaningful work—don't have renewal rituals. We don't have practice and training built into our work days; we're always performing. We just spend and spend and spend, and then we eventually burn out, or we develop unhealthy coping mechanisms, or our relationships suffer. But if we really want to maximize our contribution to the world, we need to push ourselves hard, and then give ourselves opportunities to rest, renew, and restore, so that we can come back even stronger.

By the way, vacations (which have all kinds of other benefits and value) rarely count as rest, renewal, and restoration. Too often, they require such intense preparation and so much catch-up work that any rest value evaporates. By all means, use your vacation time, if you're lucky enough to have it, but don't expect a week on the slopes or at the beach to substitute for intentional rest, renewal and restoration. Meditation (in all its forms, including the active ones), yoga, exercise, reading for pleasure, cuddling with loved ones, and savoring healthy food are all examples of what works, depending on your preferences and abilities.

Of course, alongside creating rituals and rhythms in your life that allow for alternating stress and renewal, you also need to take care of the basics. Drink plenty of water. Get the right amount of sleep for your body. Eat well. Move your body.

This might all sound basic and like it has no place in a book about employee engagement, but you're no good to others if you're not managing your own energy and taking care of yourself. There are no awards for suffering; only for doing good work.

So please, take care of yourself, my dear gardener. We need you.

To drive the message home, here's a little poem, from me to you:

You are *not* lazy

If you need 5 minutes of downtime before your next meeting.

You are *not* lazy

If you need to take a walk.

You are *not* lazy

If you need to take some deep breaths.

You are *not* lazy

If you take a lunch break.

You are *not* lazy

If you take a nap.

You are *not* lazy

If an 8-hour workday is sometimes more than you can effectively manage.

You are *not* lazy

If sometimes you just don't want to work.

And even if you *are lazy,*

It doesn't make you a bad person.

You are worth more than your productivity.

~ 9 ~

ENABLE

*Illustration by Chantel
Botha*

**In a humancentric workplace, we make sure we all
have the knowledge, tools, resources, and skills we need
to make our greatest contributions.**

*I don't want to seem indulgent
When I discuss my lows and my highs
My demise and my uprise
Pray to god I just open enough eyes
Later on, gave you the supplies and the tools
To hopefully use that'll make you strong enough to
Lift yourself up.*
—*EMINEM* "GUTS OVER FEAR"

B y now, you've laid all the groundwork to support the choice your fellow humans will make to engage with the work to be done, or to exit for a situation that is better aligned with their personal missions and goals. You have listened and developed deep empathy for your fellow humans' experiences in the workplace. Through that, you've come to understand what they need to be successful and what's getting in their way.

You've then invited your fellow humans to get involved and participate in pursuing an envisioned future and supporting your organization's most important priority. You've asked for their suggestions on how best to tackle the challenges before them, and you've gotten out of their way so that they can contribute. Through that process, you've learned the valuable lesson that, while you're pretty awesome on your own, you and your fellow humans are even stronger, smarter, and more capable together.

Having empathized with and encouraged your fellow humans, you've then climbed into a kayak of education with them. You've worked together to develop a shared understanding of what's most important, why it's important now, and what part each of your fellow humans will play in pursuing that top priority. Along the way, you've explored your own responses to key questions and developed greater empathy for your fellow humans' diverse perspectives, experiences, and responsibilities.

From here, your job as a formal or informal leader in your organization (Remember, we're defining a leader as anyone who works to bring out the best in their fellow humans, and since you're reading this book, I'm pretty sure that's you!) is to turn what you've learned about your fellow humans into action. They've taught you a great deal, and now it's time for you to respond to what you've learned by being of service to them. The fourth E, Enable, and the fifth E, Empower, focus on making sure that it's easy for your fellow humans to make their greatest contributions and become the best versions of themselves at work.

Enabling excellence

The fourth E focuses on equipping your fellow humans with the knowledge, tools, skills, and resources they'll need to be successful. You're asking them to adopt new attitudes, mindsets, and behaviors, and it's your responsibility to ensure they can.

Over the decades, I've worked with countless leaders who've wanted to "raise the bar" on employee performance. This particularly bit of corporatespeak usually means that leaders want employees to achieve more, improve metrics, and work harder—through sheer force of will, determination, and imagination—without much support from those leaders.

In a way, I get it. After all, none of us, as individuals or organizations, can assume we're at the apex of our potential right now. None of us can look at our personal or professional development and say, "Yep. That's it. I'm done." We're not done. We're always learning, growing, developing, changing. Of course, this doesn't mean we should blindly pursue more and more accomplishments, but rather, that we purposefully and consciously pursue growth and learning to become the best versions of ourselves, and to contribute to this world that sustains us.

So it's understandable that leaders want to "raise the bar" on performance in the workplace. However, if we leaders want our fellow humans to be able to reach that higher bar, we also need to raise the floor. That's what Enable is all about. We raise the floor by making sure that our fellow humans have what they need to be successful in the future we envision. If we really want them to attain higher levels of performance, we need to equip them for the task.

The good news about Enable is that, if we've done the hard work up to this point, we don't have to guess what our fellow humans need; they will have told us while we were tackling the first E, Empathize. You left Empathize (for now, of course, because you'll return later; the 6 Es are a circle, not a straight line) with a clear understanding of what your fellow humans need to be successful, and now all you have to do is give it to them.

I don't mean, though, to minimize the hard work required to make sure that each of your fellow humans in the workplace has the knowledge, tools, skills, and resources they need. None of this work is easy. And you won't be able to magically equip and enable everyone all at once. You'll need to prioritize and make incremental progress. You'll need to figure out which needs to meet first and build on each little success.

A great bonus of Enable is that it closes part of the loop of Empathize by moving from listening to action, and closing loops is the foundation for accountability and trust in any organization. Renowned relationship expert Esther Perel once said, "Trust isn't earned; it's built." And you're building trust with Enable. You're demonstrating that you listened carefully and that you can be trusted to follow through on your commitments.

I once worked in a large company in which every employee had their own office, but the organization had decided that moving them to low-walled cubicles would increase collaboration and, thereby, effectiveness. Let's put aside arguments about open vs. closed workspaces for the sake of this story. The decision was made, and it was my responsibility to "manage the change."

One of the first steps we took was to ask employees what they would need to be successful in this new environment. After all, they were being asked to perform in a dramatically transformed context, so it was reasonable to expect that what they would need to succeed in that new context might be different.

To my surprise, one of the most-commonly cited concerns that my fellow humans expressed was vulnerability. For many years, they'd grown used to having doors that closed, and to knowing that if someone was coming to visit them, they'd knock first. In an open cubicle, the nagging feeling that someone was going to sneak up behind them occupied an almost reptilian part of their brains in ways that were sure to impact their focus and effectiveness, as well as their sense of safety. To address this, we ordered convex rearview mirrors that mounted easily on employees' monitors. These gave them a way of focusing on their work while enabling them to monitor the area behind them for encroaching guests.

This is a small-but-nontrivial example of Enable. Employees were being asked to change the way they worked, so management asked them what they needed to be successful and met their needs. Notice in this story that employees didn't say, "I need a rearview mirror for my cubicle." Empathize and Enable worked together, in that case, to translate employees' stated needs and concerns (a need for privacy, a concern about unexpected visitors) into a simple solution that equipped them to perform in an environment of new expectations. The bar was raised, but so was the floor.

Enable isn't just about rearview mirrors, of course. It's also about removing friction that makes it difficult for your fellow humans to do what they need—and want—to do in support of the organization's vision, mission, and goals. Two of the most overlooked opportunities to enable employees are organization and communication.

Organize to Enable

The structure of departments and teams, especially in hierarchical (i.e., most) organizations, can create enormous friction, making it difficult for interdependent humans to work together to achieve a common goal. Everyone who has worked in an organization larger than about five employees complains about the frustrations and inefficiencies of so-called silos. One leader I knew sardonically referred to them as "cylinders of excellence." And it's true: walled-off departments that operate in a vacuum with the illusion of independence and without collaborating with others create massive organizational ineffectiveness and inefficiency.

But silos aren't really the problem. Specialization in organizations enables the development of expertise, focus on specific areas of responsibility, and, sometimes, greater productivity. The problems in modern workplaces as they relate to silos are: (1) the illusion of independence, and (2) a lack of permeability.

The illusion of independence occurs when each department in an organization believes it's the most important and that it can be successful without the others. I once worked with a global nonprofit that was troubled by interdepartmental friction. While individual teams worked well, they didn't collaborate with others. The organization was plagued by the ineffectiveness and inefficiency of one department complaining about the other and by teams throwing work "over the wall" without providing context. Petty grievances and misunderstandings grew into massive organizational dysfunction that compromised the mission and prevented employees from becoming the best versions of themselves.

At the client's request, I worked with each department individually, at first. In our kickoff workshops together, I led with a simple poll: Which is the most important organ in the human body? Their options were: brain, heart, lungs, or skin. After folks had provided their answers, I asked them to get into groups, based on the organ they'd selected, and to provide a defense for why that organ was most important.

It's absurd, of course. We all know that the human body is a complex, interdependent network of organs and organelles that are only valuable when they work together. When they stop working together, or start working against each other, the body fails.

But in organizations, you hear people argue for the importance of their specific department all the time. A salesperson says, "No one would have any work to do here if I didn't sell stuff." A product designer says, "No one would have anything to sell if I didn't create products." A line worker or software developer says, "No one would have anything to sell if I didn't make the products." An accountant says, "No one would have a job here if I didn't pay our suppliers and employees."

The truth is that they're all right, but they're all wrongheaded. From our privileged view here on the page, we can clearly see how all these functions depend on one another to create and deliver value, but when you're inside the machine, you can often become so focused on your particular set of gears that you fail to see how they connect to other parts to make the machine work.

Effective leaders often diagnose this silo problem, but they often misidentify the solutions. I can't count the number of times I've been asked: "How can we tear down silos in our organization?" The goal shouldn't be to eliminate the silos, but to make them more permeable. The modern organization is complex, dynamic, adaptive, and, above all, interdependent. In Educate, employees will begin to understand how each of their silos connects with the others to deliver value to customers. In Enable and Empower, the work is to make sure that value flows through the silos and out to customers with minimal friction.

Making silos permeable often starts with leadership. Again, assuming an organization is hierarchical, there's usually a leader at the top of the silo. That leader has their own priorities, goals, metrics, and targets to achieve. Often, their compensation is tied to what they achieve relative to those goals, metrics, and targets. This leads to overidentification with their group ("My department is 'us' and everyone else is 'them'" and siloed thinking ("The goals of other departments aren't my problem"). Over time, the department becomes saturated with that overidentification and siloed thinking—with a very narrow sense of who "we" are and a very broad sense of who "they" are. This leads to rigid and impermeable silos, to very strong teams within weak organizations. To increase the permeability of silos, leaders might need to trade a bit of their hierarchical power for more organizational effectiveness.

Patrick Lencioni examines this problem in his landmark book *Five Dysfunctions of a Team,* in which he makes "inattention to results" the peak of a pyramid of what goes wrong in leadership teams. To be clear, Lencioni is referring to inattention to overall organizational results. Leaders who become too attentive to their own group's results and take their eyes off shared results inadvertently create impermeable silos. In *The Advantage,* Lencioni expands on the problem:

> *Too many leaders seem to have a greater affinity for and loyalty to the department they lead rather than the team they're a member of and the organization they are supposed to be collectively serving. Other distractions include a concern for individual career development, budget allocations, status, and ego...*

Some of those last points reveal a deeper dysfunction in most organizations and in the broader culture: individualism as a religion. But that's a topic for another book (I say that a lot, don't I?).

To create more permeable silos, a leadership team needs clear, collective goals. We are all gardeners in the same garden, and we need to be focused on the overall health of the garden, not just our row. If one gardener is focused solely on the yield of onions, they're likely to create challenges for the gardener who is focused on the corn. But if both gardeners are focused on the clear, collective goal of making a delicious salsa, they'll work together—and with the gardeners responsible for the tomatoes, peppers, and herbs—to cultivate a garden optimized for salsa, not just for onions or corn (yes, I like corn in my salsa).

What's the salsa in your organization? Maybe it's customer satisfaction. Maybe it's social impact. Maybe it's old-fashioned revenue or profitability. Whatever it is, it takes priority over any individual gardener's goals, and it can only be made through interdependence and collaboration. A focus on clear, collective goals makes silos permeable. Beans, corn, and squash are commonly referred to as "the three sisters" because they all thrive best when planted together.

Communicate to Enable

Communication is one of the most critical activities to reduce friction for interdependent humans in the workplace. Here too, organizations often inadvertently make this difficult. How do your fellow humans communicate with each other today? How do they communicate with customers? With suppliers? With the community?

If your organization is like most, you've codified and ossified a handful of approaches that don't meet the changing, dynamic needs of today's workplace. Ask your youngest fellow humans and they'll tell you that email is a cluttered mess.

Ask your oldest and they'll tell you that Slack is a nightmare of distractions.

This isn't a book about corporate communications, so we won't get bogged down in the myriad options available today, but the point is that removing friction from communication in your organization is a critical element to enable engagement. How might you make it easier for your fellow humans in the workplace to know what they need to know when they need to know it? What tools and processes might you need? The answers will differ based on your unique circumstances.

Over years of carpenter-style management and doing things *to* our fellow humans at work, most organizations have developed very strong muscles for *controlling* information, and the gardener muscles that focus instead on *sharing* information have atrophied. This means that shifting our approach to communication so that it creates organizational conversations is going to be a workout. Don't worry though—I think you're totally up for it.

To communicate in a way that enables your fellow humans in the workplace to make their greatest contributions, keep these three principles in mind:

- Communication is always a two-way process. Simply sending a message isn't communication. We can't call it "effective communication" unless it is received and understood with approximately the same meaning as what was sent.

- Timeliness and relevance in communication are key. Getting the right message to the right people in the right medium at the right time is the goal.
- When in doubt, overcommunicate. One of my favorite articles on this topic is Patty Azzarello's "Why People Don't Do What You Say," in which the leadership communication expert expands on the old advice that we humans need to hear a message seven times to understand it by saying that we need those seven exposures to occur in three different ways, for a total of 21 times, before we're likely to act on it. If that sounds like overkill, consider how many times you've been told a tomato is a fruit.

In our garden, communication is like pollination. It spreads ideas, connects interdependent humans and teams, and makes silos work together.

Enable in action

When COVID-19 sent many office workers home in March 2020, I received multiple questions from managers about how to keep employees motivated and productive, now that they weren't in the office. This was the wrong question. In fact, you might recognize it as a variation on, "How do we engage employees?" which I hope we've established is also the wrong questions.

In 2020, many office workers were more motivated while working in the comfort and safety of their own homes than they had been when they had to commute to an office. We now know that most office workers were also more productive at home, especially in those early months, because they'd been freed from all the distractions and interruptions of an office environment. Of course, home has its own distractions and interruptions, especially for caregivers of any kind, but for the most part, businesses were reporting productivity had stayed the same or even improved. In November 2021, more than a year and a half into the pandemic, international consulting and professional services firm PwC conducted a global survey of almost 4,000 business and HR leaders, and found that productivity and performance continued to rise.

Unfortunately, that same survey found that only 30% of those leaders responding to the survey believed their firms were building high levels of trust. One of the ugliest manifestations of that lack of trust was the rise of surveillance. Some employers started focusing on technological ways to monitor employee activity (which they mistakenly labeled "productivity"), and software companies leapt into the fray to provide all kinds of ways to spy on employees, create an atmosphere of distrust, and inadvertently encourage cheating. Employees who felt they were being spied on found ways to fool the software and game the system because they felt disrespected and dehumanized. Early on, I heard the story of one employee who, once he found out software was tracking his keyboard and mouse activity, set an alarm to remind him to move his mouse at various times throughout the day. He put more energy into tricking the spyware than he put into doing his work, and the blame for the decreased productivity could be placed squarely at his employer's feet. Of course, that was before some mad genius invented the mouse-jiggler to save him the trouble.

The organizations that really impressed me during those early weeks were the ones who asked how they could *enable* their employees' productivity now that they were no longer in the office. What equipment should they make sure their employees have? Should they provide ergonomic evaluations for employees' home workspaces? Some leveraged internal ticketing systems so that home-bound employees could request equipment they needed, like monitors or standing desks. Others simply provided employees with a monetary allowance to spend on outfitting their home offices.

The approach of these progressive organizations is Enable in action. It's a mindset shift from *tracking* employees to *backing* employees, and while the data are hard to find, I'd wager that those employees were much more likely to feel emotionally connected and committed to their work and to their workplaces than those who were being spied on.

How will you Enable?

You've come a long way in this book, and I want to congratulate you for sticking with it. The ideas in this book might run counter to many that we've either been taught or absorbed in organizations that are stuck in thinking that originates in the 19th and 20th centuries, so they can be difficult to embrace. Maybe you're not there yet, but if you've made it this far, you can, at least, see the possibilities that these new approaches enable.

The old ways were based in an oppressive mindset of manipulating, coercing, and generally getting people to do stuff. The oldest ways manipulated through violence and aggression. This was followed by the rewards and punishment of the behavioralists and the "human relations" set. Later, this evolved into subtler forms of trickery and gamification, all geared toward getting our fellow humans to do things they didn't want to do.

The new way—the way of the 6 Es—is a partnership between leaders (who are, again, anyone who's working to bring out the best in their fellow humans) and their fellow humans in the workplace. It's a collaboration that cultivates more-humancentric organizations, contributes to a more just, equitable, and inclusive world, and enables better outcomes of all sorts.

Speaking of Enable, what steps can you take, regardless of your position in the organization, to "raise the floor" and to make it easier for your fellow humans to go above and beyond? You've listened and empathized. You've involved and educated. And now, it's time to Enable. Before you move on to the next chapter, I encourage you to take a moment to reflect on the following questions.

1. What attitudes, mindsets, and behaviors do I hope to see from my fellow humans in the workplace?

2. What tools, skills, or resources might make it easier for my fellow humans to adopt those attitudes, mindsets, and behaviors?

3. What opportunities do I see to reduce friction for my fellow humans in the workplace?

~ 10 ~

INTERLUDE: CULTIVATING A BIGGER SENSE OF "WE"

We're not completely ready to leave the problem of organizational silos behind. When business units, departments, and teams don't cooperate, don't trust one another, and steal cupcakes from each other's break rooms, organizational dysfunction isn't the only outcome.

Heavily siloed organizations can't solve meaningful problems. They're unable to respond efficiently and effectively to external threats or opportunities. They can't deliver their full potential value to suppliers, customers, shareholders, employees—or any other humans. They aren't nimble, flexible, or adaptable, and they sure as heck aren't agile.

At the root of all this is what I've come to call a "narrow sense of 'We.'"

A narrow sense of "We" in the workplace

As we discussed earlier, our sense of We at work often starts and ends with our immediate team or department. As employees, this narrow sense of We can cause us to over-identify with our team and under-identify with our company, our industry, or with our ecosystem of suppliers, customers, shareholders, coworkers, and communities. As leaders, a narrow We might mean over-identifying with our peers and viewing the rest of our company as They.

When our sense of We is narrow, our sense of They is correspondingly broad. When was the last time you spoke with frustration about a They within your own company? Maybe it's that team you just know isn't working as hard as your team. Perhaps it's management, who never seems to want to work with the union. Maybe it's senior leaders in your company, who are thoroughly out of touch with your day-to-day reality. Or, if you're one of those senior leaders, maybe it's those continually griping employees who don't get the big picture.

This "We-versus-They" talk might seem harmless enough. It might even make your We stronger. After all, a common enemy (i.e., a shared definition of They) has a way of strengthening our internal alliances.

But a narrow sense of We has real costs and consequences. A narrow sense of We means we don't share a vision for the future with They. We don't share a sense of purpose or even shared standards for how we treat one another. It might mean We focus on the status and health of our team at the expense of another team, of the whole organization, or even of the community. When the We is overly strong, we also tend to make broad generalizations about They, which can lead us down a path of exclusion and discrimination. In this environment, the We achieves less, operating with a counterproductive siege mentality, defending our turf, protecting our status, and suffering from all the stress and negative emotions that go along with that.

If we want to achieve great things at work, to solve challenging and meaningful problems, to live and work in constructive cultures, to become the best versions of ourselves—culture gardeners like us must cultivate a broader sense of We.

A narrow sense of "We" in the world

The subculture of our workplace is in continual dialogue with the culture of the society in which we live. The beliefs, assumptions, and expectations we cultivate at work cross over into our social worlds and spill over onto our closest friends and family members. Just as we rarely completely leave our personal lives at the office door, we carry work with us into our personal lives as well. Don't buy it? Just think about the last time you had another maddeningly frustrating conversation with your boss, then honked at too many people on your drive home.

Undoubtedly, the We-versus-They problem extends far beyond the workplace. You don't have to spend more than a few minutes on social media to find narrow We's jousting at broader They's, often with colorful language and animated GIFs that reject anything that might unite them as a single We. When we continuously live in a state of aggressively (or passively) defending our We from an imagined They, we use up vital emotional, psychological, and physical energy that we might otherwise channel into more-constructive efforts — like registering to vote, creating art, volunteering for a worthy cause, or reading (or writing) a book.

If we can begin to broaden the sense of We at work, maybe we can also expand our sense of We in the world, thereby healing at least some of the divisions that threaten to tear us apart.

But where the heck do we start?

How to cultivate a bigger We

As we discussed earlier, we first have to recognize that, at work, silos exist for a reason. Just as cells and organs in our body specialize in certain functions, so do teams and departments within organizations. We also have to accept that a healthy tension between the growth engines and the controls within a company—between the accelerators and the brakes—will always exist. Legal, for example, will never be motivated by the same factors as Sales. This isn't inherently bad or unhealthy, but simply specialization.

Second, we need to understand how silos are hurting or helping. Here, a structured diagnostic tool (like the Organizational Culture and Organizational Effectiveness Instruments from Human Synergistics, which I use with my clients) can help us examine two relevant outcomes:

- How collaborative and supportive our fellow humans are as they get work done within their own teams, i.e., how strong our silos are
- How much our fellow humans coordinate across teams to get work done in a smooth and streamlined way, i.e., how permeable, connected, and consciously interdependent our silos are

In my experience, silos in most organizations are strong and impermeable, i.e., teamwork is pretty good within silos, and coordination among silos is pretty crummy. Maybe this is a side effect of all of those years focused on "team-building," or perhaps it comes from a deeply ingrained need to identify We and They. To which group do I belong? And which groups do I think will try to steal my cupcakes? Or maybe it's a consequence of hierarchical organizational structures that motivate leaders to narrow their sense of We.

A shared understanding for a bigger We

Regardless of what's driving this strong and impermeable sense of We, if we want a more constructive workplace culture, we next need to align these separate departments as a We. One helpful ingredient for cooking up a strong We is a shared sense of purpose. In our bodies, the cells and organs must align with a common purpose, which is, ideally, keeping us healthy and alive. In a company, employees need to understand the big goals we're trying to achieve, the big vision we're trying to attain, or the big mission we're trying to fulfill — and then we all need to understand how our individual daily actions contribute to this big Why. Sound familiar? Yep, that's Educate! Educate provides the big Why that cultivates a bigger We.

As we work to broaden the sense of We in our organizations, we'll probably need to remind ourselves that the goal isn't to eliminate those reviled cylinders of excellence. The goal is to align them, connect them, and make them as permeable as possible so that they can work together to achieve the big Why. This results in a broader sense of We, one that encompasses, at least, the whole organization. For even more significant impact, that sense of We can be expanded to include suppliers, customers, shareholders, and communities by finding the big Why that matters to all and to which all contribute. I might suggest "human flourishing" as a shared goal to start with, but I encourage you to find you own if that doesn't feel right.

With a broader sense of We, we create a more constructive culture in which we can all contribute more, make a greater impact — and maybe even make the world a better place. We are all humans. We all have needs, aspirations, fears, and motivations. Some of them are universal and shared, while some are individual and unique. But what makes us We is that We all have them.

We won't cultivate a bigger We by debating about issues and philosophies. Instead, it's our stories, our emotions, our needs, aspirations, fears, and motivations that connect and permeate the silos. When we look for ways to connect through shared understanding of what's important, why it's important, and how each of us contributes, We become stronger and capable of more.

~ 11 ~

EMPOWER

Illustration by Chantel Botha

In humancentric workplaces, we make it easy for our fellow humans to do the right thing and contribute their unique genius to the problems and opportunities we face.

"What gets measured gets managed - even when it's pointless to measure and manage it, and even if it harms the purpose of the organisation to do so."

—SIMON CAULKIN

B efore we get started with the 5th E, Empower, can I just throw up a buzzword alert?

I mean, that word, empower, has become increasingly common in boardrooms and offsite workshops throughout the corporate world. Unfortunately, the more common a word becomes in the corporate world, the more it loses any significance or meaning. Lame corporate mission statements are filled with cliches about empowering customers, empowering employees, and even empowering markets. Ugh. But when I talk to managers in organizations and push them, they'll frequently admit that employees are not empowered. Quite the contrary, employees are rule-bound, constrained, and limited. The same is true for customers, who have to follow processes prescribed by rigid service providers and play by rules that make sense to the company, but not to them.

So let's get real. At the beginning of this book, I promised not to bullshit you, and that includes avoiding empty jargon. When I use the word "empower," I mean something very specific and significant. Here's how I define empower.

Em-pow'-er (verb): to make it easy for our fellow humans to make their greatest contribution to the organization, often by examining metrics, policies, and processes for unintended negative consequences, or by implementing new metrics, policies, and processes

If you remember nothing else, remember that Empower, the potent sister of Enable, makes it easy for our fellow humans to bring their maximum awesomeness to bear. Empower is not, as its etymology might imply, about giving power to people; our fellow humans already have power (though organizations and institutions frequently limit it, inadvertently or, um, advertently). Instead, it's about moving crap out of their way that has blunted or diminished their power in the workplace.

It's a shame the things that organizations do to the humans who make them exist. We spend countless hours and dollars finding just the right people to hire, people with impressive experience, deep expertise, proven abilities, and unique perspectives. Once they're on board, we force them into job descriptions, roles, hierarchies, rules, and procedures that limit the amount of value they can contribute to the organization. If Empower involves *giving* anything, it's giving *back* to our fellow humans the intrinsic power to which they're entitled after non-humancentric management approaches attempted to pick it from their pockets like a street thief.

Of course, we don't mean to do this. Those job descriptions, roles, hierarchies, rules, procedures, and metrics were put in place to maximize efficiency, ensure compliance, and reduce risk, and sometimes, they succeed, but at a cost. That's why Empower is all about understanding unintended negative consequences and perverse results.

The doctrine of unintended consequences

Throughout the speculative fiction of Margaret Atwood, the doctrine of unintended consequences is a prevalent theme. Whether it's the genetic experimentation in *Oryx and Crake,* or the social experimentation of *The Handmaid's Tale,* Atwood is masterful at tracing our best intentions as humans to their logical extents, which usually yield disastrous drawbacks.

If you've spent any time at all working in organizations, you know that unintended consequences don't just appear in fiction; they're an everyday fact of organizational life. Granted, they might not be as vivid or dire as they are in Atwood's novels, but they're destructive all the same. In the customer service center, scripts are intended to ensure consistency and professionalism, but end up frustrating customers because of their rigidity and lack of humanity. In sales, our fellow humans work hard to sell as much as possible, without regard for how their orders will be filled or supported. Throughout the organization, well-intentioned people develop dysfunctional behaviors to drive a metric that was put in place to monitor healthy functioning. Or, as we mentioned in the last chapter, software implemented to monitor employee productivity ends up reducing productivity as employees find ways to trick it.

The work of Empower

Just as with the previous four Es, the fifth E requires work, and as with all the other Es, the foundation of that work is your top strategic priority. What is it that you absolutely must become or accomplish right now? What problem must you solve? What opportunity must you approach? What must your organization be for its customers, employees, suppliers, and community? And what's getting in the way?

On top of this foundation, determine what outcomes you might need your fellow humans to work toward. What attitudes, mindsets, and behaviors will be required to achieve those outcomes? And what prevents your fellow humans from adopting them? And what will help your fellow humans experience more satisfaction, fulfillment, self-actualization, and flourishing?

With those questions in mind, it's time to examine the key policies, processes, and metrics that govern your organization's operations. Are these all working as designed, or are they generating unintended outcomes that are obstacles for your fellow humans, preventing adoption of the required attitudes, mindsets, and behaviors, standing in the way of desired outcomes, and ultimately, slowing or halting progress toward what your organization needs to achieve or become?

Customer service centers often provide multiple examples of unintended consequences and opportunities to empower. Supervisors tell agents that providing excellent customer service is the top priority. However, when the time comes for a coaching conversation, agents are evaluated based on the length of their calls (the shorter the better) and on compliance with scripts. Or they're given very little latitude to satisfy customers, as evidenced by low approval limits, for example, and have to escalate customers to supervisors who are authorized to solve real customer problems.

Many policies in organizations arise to legislate against negative events that almost never happen. One day, one employee allowed a customer to return something for a refund that the store didn't even sell, so now that store requires all returns to be approved by management. Unfortunately, while the bad thing almost never happens, our fellow humans (both employees and customers) are forced to labor under the restraints of the policy at all times.

The work, then, is to evaluate metrics, policies, and processes for ways in which they act as obstacles to our stated objectives. In some cases, the work of Empower is also to implement new policies, processes, and metrics that explicitly remove obstacles to the mindsets, attitudes, and behaviors your organization needs.

And, as with Enable, you won't have to guess what obstacles are impeding your fellow humans' success. If you've followed the guidance of the 6 Es, your fellow humans will have told you what's getting in their way, whether it's policies, processes, or metrics. Your job, now, is to remove barriers and, if necessary, grease the skids with empowering policies that make it easy for your fellow humans to adopt the attitudes, mindsets, and behaviors that will enable them to make their greatest contributions, and help your organization attain its vision, fulfill its mission, and achieve its goals.

Empower in action

One of the most famous examples of Empower in action comes from the international hotel brand Ritz-Carlton. This organization asks all of its employees, regardless of their position, to commit to a list of values that amounts to an inventory of desired attitudes, mindsets, behaviors, and outcomes. Here are just a few:

- I am always responsive to the expressed and unexpressed wishes and needs of our guests.
- I am empowered to create unique, memorable and personal experiences for our guests.
- I understand my role in achieving the Key Success Factors and creating The Ritz-Carlton Mystique.
- I create a work environment of teamwork and lateral service so that the needs of our guests and each other are met.
- I am involved in the planning of the work that affects me.
- I am proud of my professional appearance, language and behavior.
- I am responsible for uncompromising levels of cleanliness and creating a safe and accident-free environment.
- I own and immediately resolve guest problems.

Now, I don't work for Ritz-Carlton, and I've never even been a guest in one of their hotels, so I might not appreciate what all of this means. For example, I have no idea what "The

Ritz-Carlton Mystique" is, and I confess I'm a little titillated by it. However, when I view this list through the lens of the 6 Es, I can clearly see how the organization seeks to involve (Encourage) and educate (Educate) the humans who make it work, and how the organization must also take steps to Enable, Empower, and Embrace the attitudes, mindsets, behaviors, and outcomes this list enumerates.

But of most interest for Empower is this pledge: "I own and immediately resolve guest problems." I've worked in and with many organizations in which management has called for employees to "own" issues, and even to act as "owners" of the company, while at the same time tying human hands with policies and processes that make ownership impossible.

"Own that problem," they seem to say, "but make sure you hand it off to accounting at this step to ensure compliance." Or, "Own that issue until it's resolved, but remember that you're only allowed to approve customer credits up to 25 dollars." Or, "Own it, but make sure your conversation with the customer doesn't take longer than three minutes and 24 seconds."

Ritz-Carlton quite famously handles things differently, giving every employee, regardless of role, the ability to spend up to 2000 US dollars per guest per day to resolve a guest problem—without asking for anyone's permission. This isn't an arbitrary policy put in place for good PR, though it does accomplish that. And the amount might've changed since last I spoke with someone at Ritz-Carlton or by the time you're reading this book, but the dollar amount isn't really the point. This policy empowers employees to deliver on their pledge, "I own and immediately resolve guest problems." It provides them with the *policy* that empowers the *pledge.*

Of course, not every organization can be Ritz-Carlton, and $2000 might be totally out of scale for your organization, but many other organizations have adapted the spirit of this policy to empower the humans who interact with customers to deliver great customer service. A multinational commercial real estate and property management company encourages all employees to spend up to $500 to take care of anyone who has an issue in one of their properties, whether they're replacing a light bulb or buying someone a new dress after it got caught in an escalator. A regional electric utility company allows the workers who maintain its power lines to spend up to $50 to do something extra for a customer when on or near their property. Policies like these go a long way toward helping the humans doing the work believe that the organization is truly committed to taking care of the humans it serves (which it probably calls "customers").

Nordstrom is also noteworthy for the approach it takes to Empower humans. Famously, Nordstrom hands every employee a card when they start that articulates the company's most-important rule: "Use good judgment in all situations. Please feel free to ask your department manager, store manager, or human resources officer any question at any time."

Another example of Empower in action is/are the policies that many organizations have put in place in recent years to support flexible work. While some organizations articulate these policies as *allowing* employees to work from locations of their choosing and at times of their choosing, I prefer to think of these policies as *removing barriers* to employee effectiveness and fulfillment. When employees have some choice in when, where, and how they work, they're better able to maximize their contribution and become the best versions of themselves in all spheres of their lives.

The topic of work flexibility deserves its own book (and there are many), but I'll just say that the choices of when, where, and how don't need to be unlimited. Pretty much anyone who has chosen to be employed by an organization knows that they won't have 100% autonomy. Flexibility is all about autonomy within constraints. Our job as leaders is simply to be clear and cogent about those constraints. Within what parameters can our fellow humans make their own choices, and what is the rationale for those parameters? Oh, and I hope this goes without saying at this point, but we probably should *involve employees* in defining those parameters.

Enable and Empower: reducing employee effort

As I said at the beginning of this chapter, Enable and Empower are sisters, a superhero duo that, instead of fighting crime, fights unnecessary effort. Let me just take a second to distinguish between them.

The discipline of Enable focuses on equipping our fellow humans with the knowledge, skills, tools, and resources they need. The practice of this discipline involves asking:

- What do you need to be successful in your work?
- What do you need to maximize the contribution you make through your work?
- What do you need to become the best version of yourself through your work?
- What knowledge, skills, tools, or resources do you need but don't currently have?

The discipline of Empower focuses on removing obstacles and making it easy for our fellow humans to do what they're here to do. The practice of this discipline involves asking:

- What's getting in your way at work?
- What's preventing you from maximizing your contribution through your work?
- What's standing in the way of becoming the best version of yourself through your work?
- What changes to policies, processes, or metrics would make it easier for you to contribute?

In the world of customer experience, folks have been measuring customer effort since about 2010, inspired in part by the Customer Effort Score that was introduced by Gartner around that time. However, measurement of employee effort has yet to come into the mainstream. In my research, I've seen indications that the level of effort employees have to expend to do their jobs is inversely related to the level of connection they feel to their work.

Gallup's famous employee engagement surveys ask respondents to rate, "I have the materials and equipment I need to do my work right," which is similar to what Enable is about, and also connects to the idea of overall employee effort. Those who respond positively to that item are much more likely to be "engaged" in Gallup's framework.

In other words, when our fellow humans don't feel enabled and empowered, they're less likely to feel engaged.

While Enable and Empower are each powerful on their own, they're even more powerful together, and a key way for leaders to demonstrate accountability, trust, and trustworthiness.

Reflecting on Empower

Wow. You've made it through five of the 6 Es! If I could, I'd throw a small, ecofriendly confetti party for you right now, but I can't, so you'll have to do that for yourself. Maybe go empty your paper shredder, toss it all up the in air, roll around naked in it for a while, and then, once you're partied out, stuff all those shreds in the compost bin to feed your garden in the spring. To be clear, I take no responsibility for papercuts.

Welcome back. Did you have a good roll in the shreds? Before you get back to business and move on to the 6th and final E, take some time to answer these questions. If you're in a place where you can do this safely, take the time to actually write down your answers. You'll want to share these ideas with your fellow humans in the workplace later.

1. Thinking back on the attitudes, mindsets, and behaviors we really need to see in our workplace, what current metrics, policies, or processes that we follow are counterproductive? Which are getting in the way and making it more difficult for us to adopt those attitudes, mindsets, and behaviors?

2. Continuing to think about those required attitudes, mindsets, and behaviors, what else could we be doing in the workplace to make them easier to adopt? Do we need to remove obstacles or do we need to build policies, processes, and metrics that support those attitudes, mindsets, and behaviors?

3. Take another look at the key metrics by which your organization measures individual performance and success, and remember that what gets measured gets managed, even when it's pointless. Are there any performance metrics or other ways in which your fellow humans are evaluated that are working *against* the future you envision and might be encouraging attitudes, mindsets, and behaviors that are counter to those we really need to see?

~ 12 ~

INTERLUDE: ABOUT
RESISTANCE

As you embark on this journey of using the 6 Es to cultivate a more authentically engaged and humancentric workplace, I have to warn you that you will encounter resistance.

Contrary to traditional change management perspectives, though, resistance isn't a bad thing. It isn't something to be avoided or squashed. In fact, resistance can be a very good thing. Since you're using the 6 Es, you're less likely to encounter vehement and violent resistance; you're more likely to find resistance in its more passive forms, like fear, reluctance, and concern.

Because I'm in your corner on this, and because I know that your mission is to make work—and the world—a better place, I feel compelled to share with you a harsh but undeniable truth: change is hard.

OK, you probably already knew that. But do you know why? Because if you know why, you might be able to find a way to make that truth a little less harsh.

David Rock is a leadership expert who, many years ago, began incorporating neuroscience into his work. His book, *Your Brain at Work,* is recommended reading for anyone who wants to understand how our brains help us and hold us back as we try to make our contributions through our work.

In 2008, Rock published an article that changed my life. If you can find "SCARF: a brain-based model for collaborating with and influencing others," I highly recommend giving it a careful read. But since you're here now, allow me to share my understanding of the SCARF model and how it can help you better lead others through change.

SCARF is based on research that Rock conducted in collaboration with neuroscientists to understand how human behavior is governed by the brain. Through the research, Rock and his partners discovered five human *social* needs that, thanks to evolution, the brain treats as if they are *survival* needs. Those five needs are:

- **Status**. The need to know where we stand in a social hierarchy, and especially to know that we're not on the bottom
- **Certainty**. The need to know what's going to happen to us next

- **Autonomy**. The need to control what happens to us next
- **Relatedness**. The need to belong to a group
- **Fairness**. The need for ourselves and others to be treated equitably

Because the brain thinks these are survival needs, any threat to them is perceived as pain, and any reward to them is perceived as pleasure. The goal at all times, then, is to minimize threats and maximize rewards for ourselves and our fellow humans. Otherwise, we go into a defensive posture that makes us less receptive to, well, much of anything.

illustration by Chantel Botha

To make this a little more vivid, imagine that you're leading a truly transformative effort in your organization. A company that has historically been focused on its own products, processes, and policies will, in a near future, become more humancentric, focused on the people it serves (a.k.a. customers), the people who enable it (a.k.a. employees), and the community in which it operates. It's a massive overhaul that will result in changes to roles, job descriptions, reporting relationships, responsibilities, success metrics, policies, technology, and business processes.

Now take another look at that bulleted list above, and think about how this change will be perceived by your fellow humans. Better yet, put yourself in the shoes of the person in the organization with the least power and think about how you would perceive this transformation, especially if it's happening *to* you, and not *with* you. You'll probably have a lot of doubts and concerns.

- Where do I stand in the new vision? Is there an opportunity for advancement or promotion, or does this feel like a demotion?
- What's gonna happen next?
- Do I have any say in my own future? Who's making the decisions that affect me?
- Will I be part of the same team? On a different team? Is the identity of our organization changing?
- Am I being treated fairly in this process? Are my fellow humans being treated fairly? Are opportunities equitable for all?

In most cases, change threatens all the elements of the SCARF model to varying degrees. And when we're in a threatened state, we aren't open to new ideas, we aren't creative, we aren't generative, and we aren't cooperative. In fact, in spite of our own intellectual processes and the attempts of our frontal lobe to take control, the back of our brain asserts itself and puts us into a self-protective mode. Needless to say, this mode isn't conducive to our forming an emotional connection and commitment to the work to be done.

So what can you do as a humancentric leader to smooth the SCARF and ensure that your fellow humans don't feel imperiled by the good work you're trying to do?

Remember that we said the goal is to minimize threats and maximize rewards to the five needs. Here are some tips to help you as you're trying to influence your fellow humans:

- **Status**. What can you do to make sure your fellow humans feel respected? How can you lift folks up? Focus on individuals' strengths and let them know how those strengths will be needed. For example, "You're really good at breaking big projects down into discrete tasks, and we're going to need help with that."
- **Certainty**. Absolute certainty in a volatile world is impossible, but communication can go a long way to soothe the uncertainty monster. Be transparent with your fellow humans about what you know, what you don't know, and when you think you'll know more. That last bit is really important: "I don't know, but I'll know more in two weeks." And don't underestimate

the power of the shared understanding that comes through Educate to quell uncertainty.

- **Autonomy**. The second E, Encourage, is a key discipline for reducing threats to autonomy. Include, involve, and invite your fellow humans. Make sure that as many as possible participate in creating the future with which you hope they'll engage.
- **Relatedness**. Allow plenty of room in the undoubtedly busy schedule for authentic human connection. Facilitate opportunities for your fellow humans to get to know one another and to create a sense of "we" within your organization. Make sure that the sense of "we" extends beyond intact teams or departments to encompass the entire organization. Even better if that "we" includes customers, suppliers, and your community. If we all feel part of the larger "we," our sense of relatedness is less vulnerable to the threats of reporting relationships and organizational structures changing.
- **Fairness**. This is perhaps the most straightforward and the most difficult to manage of Rock's five needs. Two tools to lean on together that will minimize threats and maximize rewards to fairness are: (1) transparent communication, and (2) procedural justice. Be very clear with your fellow humans about how decisions are made along the way. Of course, not all decisions can be universally popular and accepted, but when we perceive the process of arriving at those decisions as fair, our sense of fairness is rewarded.

Think back over your own experiences of "being changed," in the words of Peter Senge. I'm sure you can point to ways in which your sense of status, certainty, autonomy, relatedness, and fairness were threatened. This doesn't even have to be a major change. Think about that time yesterday when you were frustrated with a fellow human in the workplace. Was that person threatening some element of SCARF? How might you have handled the situation differently to reduce the threat for yourself? Is it possible that you were threatening some element of SCARF for that person? If so, how might you have handled the situation differently to minimize the threats and maximize rewards?

~ 13 ~

EMBRACE

Illustration by Chantel Botha

In a humancentric workplace, we reinforce, recognize, and reward the attitudes, mindsets, behaviors, and outcomes we expect of ourselves and our fellow humans.

"What's gonna set you free? Look inside and you'll see. When you've got so much to say it's called gratitude, and that's right."

BEASTIE BOYS "GRATITUDE"

L et's get the discomfort out of the way right now. The 6th E, Embrace, is a word that tends to make a lot of folks uncomfortable in the workplace. It's one of those words, like "love," that some folks just don't think belongs in the workplace.

And let's be perfectly clear: we are not talking about physical embraces with the 6th E. Unless your workplace has established norms in which physical contact like that is valued and welcomed and you have explicit consent, I am not advocating for hugging your fellow humans in the workplace, especially without asking first.

(That said, I frankly think the workplace would benefit from more hugging and love, as long as those things were truly valued, welcomed, and consensual, and no one got creepy about it.)

So what are we talking about with Embrace? We've reached the last of the 6 Es, so it must be some kind of pinnacle or zenith, right?

Well, yes, but also no. Let's not forget that the 6 Es are roughly cyclical, so while Embrace is the last E, it's also right before the first E. Crazy, right? I don't want anyone getting the mistaken impression that this is the end of the work of creating an authentically humancentric workplace. The 6 Es are disciplines to practice, not tasks to check off.

Embrace is all about consciously and conscientiously reinforcing the attitudes, mindsets, behaviors, and outcomes that are going to enable our organization to achieve what it needs to achieve and to become what it needs to become. Embrace reminds us to celebrate not just the big wins, but the small wins along the way, to appreciate the journey as much as the destination, and to notice success in all its forms.

How to Embrace

Most organizations I've worked in or with over my decades in the corporate world aren't particularly good at celebrating wins. In fact, most are so bent on continuous improvement and "raising the bar" that they hardly notice when something good has happened. They've developed really strong muscles, instincts, and processes for spotting defects and problems, but they're much weaker at seeing their opposites.

Of course, there are plenty of end-of-the-year award ceremonies, big sales prizes, President's Clubs, and all that, but those mostly focus on big outcomes, while very few focus on the steps along the way that get us there. This is probably a pitfall of always being "results-oriented" (like pretty much everyone on LinkedIn) or of our relentless focus on things we can measure or of a general privileging of product over process. Whatever it is, Embrace is a reminder to notice the incipient things, the glimmers of goodness, the hard-to-measure things, the mini-things that really matter.

Done right, Embrace should provide our fellow humans with clear, unambiguous, and targeted evidence that their attitudes, mindsets, and behaviors are encouraged and valued.

Embrace should be like those pellets that Pac-Man eats, the ones that give him the energy, speed, and enthusiasm he needs to chase ghosts and eat cherries, in spite of his being winded, a little tired of being pursued, and thinking about maybe just hiding out in the corner of the maze to play some *other* game.

Embrace is about recognition and reinforcement. Sometimes, it's also about rewards, but it doesn't always have to be. Since these words have been used interchangeably in the corporate world for a while, let's be clear about the differences. **Reinforcement** is simply anything that reminds us of the importance of something. This can include recognition and rewards. **Recognition** is the act of *recognizing* when something good has happened. This can be paired with rewards, but also has value on its own. **Rewards** are gifts that punctuate recognition. While these often take some kind of financial form (from bonuses to gift cards), organizations also reward with promotions and titles, stretch assignments, schedule flexibility, and many other non-monetary gifts.

With that bit of clarification, we understand that Embrace focuses on reinforcement, which sometimes includes recognition and rewards. To effectively Embrace your fellow humans in the workplace, make sure your reinforcements have the following characteristics:

- **Personalized.** Embrace your fellow humans in ways that are personally valuable and meaningful to them as individuals. Some folks like public recognition, while others would rather be private. Money might push the buttons for some, but others might prefer something that more closely matches their individuality, personal interests, and motivations.

- **Frequent.** In the midst of the many demands of the modern workplace, it's difficult to keep Embrace in mind, but if it only happens once in a while, it won't have the desired effect of clearly conveying that a given attitude, mindset, or behavior is encouraged and valued. If we're playing in an orchestra together, and you notice I'm consistently hitting that high A perfectly, give me a little nod every time we rehearse, not just at the big concert.

- **Relevant.** If I'm consistently hitting that high A perfectly, but there's actually no high A in the piece of music our orchestra is playing, that's not a time for Embrace. Remember those reflection questions from Enable, when you created a clear vision of the desired future and specified the attitudes, mindsets, behaviors, and outcomes you'd need to see in that future state? Those are what you want to Embrace. When you notice something that's relevant to what the organization must accomplish or who it must become, that's the time to Embrace.

- **Specific.** Most of your fellow humans are happy to repeatedly demonstrate attitudes, mindsets, and behaviors that they know are encouraged and valued, but so often, we aren't specific enough in our Embrace. Don't just say, "Good job." Instead, start with this template and make it your own:

- ○ "I noticed you _____ (specify the attitude, mindset, or behavior you noticed), which _____ (specify how this attitude, mindset, or behavior supports the organization's vision, mission, or goals), and that's important because _____ (remind your fellow human of the organization's vision, mission, or goals)."

- **Timely.** Don't wait until the monthly staff meeting or annual awards dinner to Embrace, and don't wait for something big to happen. As soon as you notice evidence of an attitude, mindset, or behavior that you want to see more of from your fellow humans, Embrace. The closer to the moment you can get, the greater your impact.

THE 5 ATTRIBUTES OF EFFECTIVE RECOGNITION

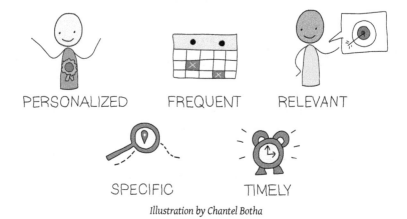

PERSONALIZED   FREQUENT   RELEVANT

SPECIFIC   TIMELY

Illustration by Chantel Botha

You're probably doing it wrong

I'm not trying to throw any shade here, but given the above description of what it takes to effectively Embrace, it's likely that your current rewards and recognition programs are falling short. That doesn't necessarily mean you should stop doing them altogether, but for maximum impact, you should pare down your Embrace efforts to those that are more likely to cultivate connection and commitment among your fellow humans.

With a few exceptions, employee-of-the-month programs (we'll use this as shorthand, though it applies to employee-of-the-week, quarter, etc.) are *not* examples of Embrace in action. These programs usually involve some kind of public recognition, maybe a plaque, and sometimes a monetary reward, which means they aren't personalized to the recipient. They're infrequent and not at all timely, by design.

Sometimes they're relevant and specific, but more often, they're based on nominations or the first name that comes to mind or the person who worked the hardest in the previous time period. They rarely point to specific attitudes, mindsets, or behaviors that connect to the organization's vision, mission, and goals. It's not that there isn't value in having an employee of the month, but if this distracts from what you really want your fellow humans to focus on, it probably isn't helping. In fact, they can even backfire with unintended consequences, such as reinforcing an organization's bias toward extroverts and against introverts, or celebrating the same "usual suspects," who are often straight, cis, non-disabled, White men.

Likewise, most years-of-service awards don't meet the Embrace criteria either. Again, it's not that recognizing your fellow humans for their tenure and thanking them for sticking around aren't valuable. But these awards aren't personalized, frequent, relevant, specific, or timely, and they also run the risk of overvaluing butt-in-chair time vs. value added to the organization. In some organizations, sticking around for 30 years isn't a sign of connection and commitment at all, but merely of persistence and endurance. It's quite possible for an employee who's been with the organization for a month to demonstrate more connection and commitment than a veteran employee has done all year—or their entire career.

Speaking of doing it wrong, many years ago, I was a new employee in a large enterprise when I was selected for a cross-functional focus group, hosted by the chief human resources officer. Being selected for that focus group could have been an opportunity for Embrace in itself, if I'd known why I was picked or how it connected to strategic priorities, but I was never given a reason for being selected. Missed opportunity number one.

I attended the focus group, offered my perspective, and was glad to have been of help. A week later, I was surprised to receive an envelope addressed to me via interoffice mail. Upon opening, the handwritten thank-you note from the CHRO herself delighted me. She wrote a few words to tell me both *what* she appreciated about my contribution to the focus group and *why* it was valuable in the context of what the company was hoping to achieve.

If my story stopped here, it would've been a decent ex-ample of Embrace—not a home run, but a respectable base hit. Unfortunately, corporate habits can often get in the way of humancentric action. Following what was likely a long-standing approach to rewards and recognition, a $5 gift card for a big-box retail store was tucked into the envelope with the thoughtful note. You can call me ungrateful in this story for not appreciating the token, but for the purposes of illustrating Embrace, indulge me in a little explanation of why this, for me, negated the Embrace value of the hand-written note.

First, anyone who knows me will tell you that I love to sup-port small and locally owned businesses. Big-box retailers serve their purpose in the community, but I'd much rather give my money to those who need it and appreciate it, and who invest it back in my local community. So the gift card was far from personalized because that's not my idea of a fulfilling shopping experience.

Second, the dollar amount, while appropriate in scale to my small contribution, didn't actually make sense at this particular retailer. If you walked into your local Tesco, Wal-Mart, or Target with just $5, and you were an adult, what would you do with it? Most likely, you'd spend much more, and the gift card would act like a $5-off coupon. If it had been $5 at, say, an ice cream shop or a bakery, it might've felt like I could have a little fun with it. So it wasn't of much practical value to me.

Again, my point isn't to relish my own lack of appreciation, but instead, to point out what makes Embrace truly effective. The CHRO probably sent those gift cards to everyone who participated, but she could've saved the company a few dollars and, more importantly, gained *more* connection and commitment by just sending the handwritten notes, which have special value coming from an executive.

Embrace in action

I worked with one large company in the US that put together a recognition program that embraced (ahem) all of the 6 Es expertly. They began by convening a group of employees to discuss what was working and what wasn't in the company's existing rewards and recognition. The focus group explored how recognition could better connect to strategic priorities, and be more personalized and frequent. In the end, the employee-led effort created a program in which employees can nominate anyone in their organization—a peer, a manager, an executive, a direct support—based on specific criteria that connect to the current priorities. A cross-functional committee of employees, with members who periodically rotate in and out, reviews nominations quarterly and selects winners. Those recipients are then able to choose from among a number of reward options, depending on what's valuable to them.

I appreciate the ways in which this program incorporated input (Empathize) and involvement (Encourage) from employees, required meaningful dialogue to develop shared understanding of priorities (Educate), and then Enabled and Empowered employees, regardless of their place in the hierarchy, to celebrate their fellow humans' attitudes, mindsets, and behaviors.

In recent years, a number of online platforms have emerged to enable timely, frequent, and personalized recognition across organizations. Some even use a peer-based recognition approach, similar to my example, and enable employees to accrue recognition "points" that they can exchange for rewards that they value.

Embrace in context

As we can see in the above example, Embrace brings all the 6 Es together. Here's how.

Like all of the Es, Embrace is not a tactic, a technique, or a step in a project; it's a discipline. Embrace reminds us to focus on connecting the dots between the current state and the future state, and to do so in a strategic and humancentric way. As a reminder, here's what those dots look like:

- **Vision.** What's the world we want to help create and be part of? What contribution will we make to that world? Why is that important?
- **Mission.** Why do we exist today? What's our passion and our purpose? If we were in a completely different industry, would our reason for existence be different?
- **Strategy.** How do we plan to approach the fulfillment of our mission and attainment of our vision? How will we organize? Where will we focus? Why?
- **Goals.** In the near-ish term, what do we need to accomplish to advance our strategy? What organizational outcomes do we need to see, and by when?
- **Behaviors.** What behaviors do we need to exhibit to achieve our goals, execute our strategy, fulfill our mission, and attain our vision?
- **Mindsets.** What thoughts, beliefs, and assumptions do we need to develop to support the behaviors we need, the goals we'll accomplish, the strategy we'll execute, the mission we'll fulfill, and the vision we'll attain?

- **Attitudes.** How do we need to feel about our work and our fellow humans so that we can meet our goals, fulfill our mission, and attain our vision?

The last three bullets—attitudes, mindsets, and behaviors—are what we need to Embrace. This isn't about treating our fellow humans like Pavlovian machines, and this goes way beyond behavioralist positive reinforcement. Embrace is a key part of executing any strategy. The ways we Embrace indicate how committed we are to achieving outcomes and making a contribution to the world.

In Embrace, we become aware, mindful, and attentive to elements of the workplace that previously went unnoticed. We notice, of course, how we and our fellow humans act, but we also begin to notice how they think and feel. And as we notice, we begin to see the actions, thoughts, and feelings that are helping us all move closer to being and accomplishing what we're here for. And when we notice, we let everyone know that we've noticed.

Yes, there's an element of positive reinforcement—reward what you want repeated—but as humancentric leaders, we know that we aren't here to manipulate our fellow humans. Instead, we're here to do meaningful work, and we want our fellow humans to be as emotionally connected and committed to that work as we are. We're gardeners, cultivating the workplace—and the world—we want live in. We want to feel valued and appreciated, so we want our fellow humans to feel valued and appreciated—not just for their instrumental value to the organization, but for who they are.

In service to our fellow humans, we use the 6 Es to cultivate the conditions that will achieve one of two equally important goals:

1. Our fellow humans will feel so emotionally connected and committed to our humancentric mission that they willingly and proactively go above and beyond to enable the organization to attain its vision, fulfill its mission, and achieve its goals, while achieving greater satisfaction, fulfillment, self-actualization, and flourishing, OR...

2. Our fellow humans realize that they don't feel emotionally connected and committed to our work, and choose to exit. Remember that this is an equally valid, positive, and humancentric outcome.

When we Embrace, we remind ourselves and our fellow humans about what's really important. Through evolution, our brains have become highly attuned to noticing the bad, the negative, and the aberrant, but Embrace trains our brains to notice the good. It refocuses us on what our fellow humans are feeling, thinking, and doing, and how those feelings, thoughts, and actions are helping us make a meaningful contribution.

When we Embrace, we add the rocket fuel of recognition to our organization's efforts, while we continue to honor our fellow humans' desire for two things:

1. To be valued and appreciated (as pointed out by management consultants Ken Blanchard and Spencer Johnson in their classic, *The One Minute Manager*), and
2. To make daily progress on meaningful work (as observed by management researchers Teresa Amabile and Steven Kramer in the *Progress Principle*)

When we Embrace, we don't just notice the good, but we celebrate it enthusiastically. While organizational processes and policies are wired for the opposite, Embrace allows us to—to borrow a phrase from Blanchard and Johnson—catch people doing something right.

Wait! Where are you going?

I get it: you finished the last of the 6 Es and figured you'd sprint to the finish line. I've been there. But as with all the 6 Es, this last one will serve you better with a bit of reflection. Before you sprint on, consider these questions:

- When was the last time someone caught me doing something right?
- When was the last time I caught someone doing something right?
- When I currently receive recognition, does it feel valuable to me?

- When I currently give recognition, am I personalizing it to the recipient?
- How frequently do I receive recognition? How frequently do I give it?
- When I receive recognition, do I clearly understand how it connects to my organization's top priority?
- When I give recognition, do I connect it to my organization's top priority?
- When I receive recognition, do I know exactly what behavior, mindset, or attitude is being valued and appreciated, and why?
- When I give recognition, do I specify what I'm appreciating and why it's valued?
- When I receive recognition, does it occur shortly after the attitude, mindset, or behavior that is being appreciated?
- Do I give recognition as soon as possible after I observe the attitude, mindset, or behavior that I appreciate?
- What do I need to do differently to give recognition that is personalized, frequent, relevant, specific, and timely?

~ 14 ~

PUTTING THE 6 ES
TOGETHER

You now know nearly as much as I know about the 6 Es, and that's awesome. But, contrary to popular belief, and with apologies to Sir Francis Bacon, Ralph Waldo Emerson, and Thomas Hobbes, knowledge itself is *not* power. Instead, I would say that knowledge *acted upon* is power.

The fact that you have read this book and that you know the 6 Es does nothing to help you and your fellow humans cultivate a humancentric workplace and make work more than just another four-letter word. Maybe this is self-evident, but I don't like to make assumptions. So consider this your call to action. Take your knowledge and do something with it, preferably today.

How to start with the 6 Es

I haven't bullshitted (bullshat?) you through this whole book, and I'm certainly not going to start now. So here's the truth: Getting started with the 6 Es isn't easy, but I'm going to walk you through it.

You probably picked up this book because you have a goal related to employee engagement. Or maybe you picked it up because your efforts to engage employees have failed. Or it could be that you picked it up because you think all this talk about employee engagement is just plain dumb. That's all good. Regardless of your reason for picking up this book, you're welcome to it.

The first mistake that most employee engagement efforts make is that they don't answer the question: Engage with what? So your first job is to answer that question, and it's a doozy.

1. What do we want our fellow humans in the workplace to engage with?

To answer this first question, we're going to need a few ingredients:

- Our vision for the future, in vivid terms, including such things as: what the organization will have accomplished, who the organization will be for its various stakeholders, what it will feel like to be part of the organization, and what it will feel like to be a customer of the organization

- The behaviors we need our fellow humans to exhibit so that our organization achieves that desired future
- The attitudes (feelings) and mindsets (thoughts) that our fellow humans will need to adopt to support the required behaviors and achieve the desired future

Once we've pulled all those ingredients together, we can move into planning mode, but I strongly urge you *not* to move forward with planning if you can't clearly answer that first question.

Remember that we aren't allowing our definition of employee engagement to be sloppy, to somehow be about satisfaction, happiness, morale, and motivation. Instead, our definition of an engaged employee is precise:

a fellow human who is so emotionally connected and committed to their work that they willingly and proactively go above and beyond their job description to help the organization attain its vision, fulfill its mission, and achieve its goals in return for the promise of increased satisfaction, fulfillment, self-actualization, and flourishing.

Read that definition again, if you need to. Commit it to memory. Scribble it on a sticky note and post it in your work-space. This definition, along with your answer to the first question, will guide everything you do.

OK, I think you're ready for the second question.

> 2. How might we better understand and empathize with our fellow humans' experiences in the workplace?

I hope you'll recognize this as the key question of **Empathize**, though it hasn't quite been presented this way. We'll likely start by reflecting on how well we currently understand and can really *feel* what it's like for our fellow humans. In most hierarchical organizations, the higher up you are, the less understanding and empathy you'll naturally have for those who are lower. This isn't a fault, and it's nothing to be ashamed of; it's merely an opportunity to improve, for ourselves and for others. At a minimum, look at Empathize as an opportunity to understand two key things:

- What knowledge, skills, tools, and resources will support my fellow humans in making their greatest contributions and becoming the best versions of themselves?
- What obstacles or sources of friction are getting in their way?

I know of one senior leader who decided the right way for him to Empathize was to meet individually with every employee in his organization. That was a *lot* of work, and it might not be the approach you take. Regardless, we'll need a plan for how we'll gather feedback that will enable us to develop understanding of and empathy for our fellow humans' work experiences, and how we'll manage to stay in touch as we practice the rest of the 6 Es. Make an ambitious-but-realistic plan, and then move on to the next question.

> 3. How might we gain greater participation and involve more of our fellow humans in planning and implementation for our organization's most important priorities?

Involvement and participation is a key ingredient in developing an emotional connection and commitment to the work to be done. Remember that people don't resist change; we resist being changed. At the same time, remember that we can't involve everyone in everything, that decision-making needs to be clear, and that participation and consensus aren't the same thing.

Encourage is a bit of a balancing act, but most organizations tilt too far in the "decide-and-announce" direction, so the likelihood that we're currently doing *too much* to involve our fellow humans in our most important priorities is pretty slim. Rather than waiting for management to solve the thorniest problems, might we solicit suggestions from the broader organization, and then invite those who make suggestions to participate in their implementation? Remember that it isn't your job to solve everything; your organization employs many people who bring their own unique experiences, expertise, gifts, strengths, and talents to work with them. Encourage is all about giving those people the opportunity to make their greatest contribution. And once we've involved them in meaningful ways, they'll be much more likely to participate in **Educate**.

> 4. How might we ensure that all our fellow humans share an understanding of our most important priorities are, why they're important now, and how they can contribute?

This question encourages us to think of Educate in terms of learning objectives, of a finish line toward which to strive, and not as something that can be solved through one-way communication campaigns and training classes. If you're a leader in the organization, you've probably developed a deep and almost unconscious understanding of your organization's top priorities, why they're important, and what your role is in pursuing them. You likely think about these things in the shower, when you're commuting, or as you're falling asleep.

But your fellow humans haven't been in your head all this time. Educate is our opportunity to put everyone's heads in the same space. Like the 6 Es themselves, Educate is an ongoing process, not an event, so while we might make a plan for the first round, we'll also need to recognize that it has no end until all of our fellow humans have a shared understanding regarding our organization's top priorities, and each individual has a clear understanding of the attitudes, mindsets, behaviors, and outcomes they'll need to support those priorities. Understanding, however, won't be all they'll need.

5. How might we ensure that all our fellow humans have the knowledge, tools, skills, and resources they need to succeed?

When we ask our fellow humans to go above and beyond, we're raising the bar, and the ethical and effective step to take in support of that is to raise the floor. We'll take what we've learned from the Empathize discipline (including on-going listening) to make sure that our fellow humans have what they need to succeed.

The work of **Enable** includes evaluating the tools (digital and analog) that employees use to do their work, as well as the organizational structure, communication tools and proto-cols, and the skills that are required. Often in organizations, the performance management process blames our fellow humans for poor performance, but doesn't provide sufficient support for those humans. Enable shifts the mindset from *tracking* employees to *backing* employees, from viewing em-ployees as a homogeneous collection of objects to be acted upon to assuming that our fellow humans are whole people, just like us, and that they might simply need knowledge, tools, skills, or resources to perform at the expected level of full engagement. Enable is the superhero sister of **Empower**.

6. How might we make it easy for our fellow humans to go above and beyond in support of the organiza-tion's top priorities? How might we grease the skids or remove barriers to success?

Once again, we'll take what we learned from **Empathize** and ongoing listening to reduce friction and make it as easy as possible for our fellow humans to adopt the attitudes, mindsets, and behaviors that are needed. We'll find and fix metrics, policies, and processes that have unintended consequences or that send mixed messages to our fellow humans. We might find opportunities to add new policies or processes that more effectively support our desired future.

With Empower, we'll acknowledge that some of the limitations to employee engagement are built into the organization, and will need to be remodeled if we want to increase engagement. When we take action to address these barriers, our fellow humans will feel a greater emotional connection and commitment to the work to be done, and to the organization, and they'll be more likely to exhibit the attitudes, mindsets, and behaviors—and to achieve the outcomes—we hope for.

> 7. How might we reinforce, recognize, or reward the attitudes, mindsets, behaviors, and outcomes that we need—to achieve what we need to achieve or to become what we need to become?

With **Embrace**, we will commit to recognizing not just positive achievements and outcomes, but also their leading indicators, which are the attitudes, mindsets, and behaviors that we and our fellow humans need in order to flourish in our envisioned future. We'll understand each of our fellow humans as individuals so that we can make sure our recognition is personalized, frequent, relevant, specific, and timely.

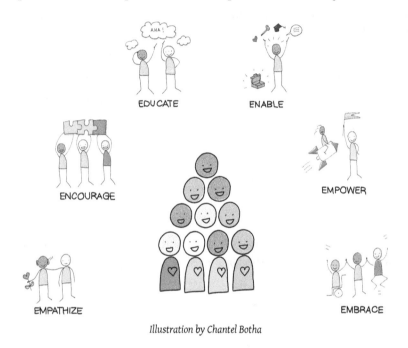

Illustration by Chantel Botha

Time to get to work

I sincerely want to applaud you for taking on this mission of creating a more-humancentric workplace: a place in which each of your fellow humans can use their strengths and gifts to make their maximum contribution and become the best versions of themselves—a place in which work is more than just another four-letter word.

Humancentric workplaces are a key building block for a humancentric society, one in which each person is respected

and valued, both as an individual and as part of a constructive collective.

As we part ways, I encourage you to contemplate one last set
of reflection questions to make the 6 Es real for you:

- Why is a humancentric workplace important to me?
  Why now?
- What assumptions do I have about my fellow humans?
  How are those assumptions limiting what's possible?
  How are they helping?
- When I think about my fellow humans in the workplace, what are some of the first words that come to
  mind?
- What steps can I take immediately to increase my empathy for and understanding of my fellow humans in
  the workplace?
- What steps can I take immediately to involve my fellow
  humans in addressing our organization's top strategic
  priority?
- What steps can I take to develop a shared understanding throughout my organization of what's most important, why it's important now, and what each person's
  role is in pursuit of that priority?
- How can I make sure that my fellow humans have the
  knowledge, skills, tools, and resources they need to
  succeed?
- What barriers to success can I help remove?

- How can I be more consistent and effective in showing my fellow humans that they are valued and appreciated?
- What might be possible if I take action related to all of the above that isn't possible right now?

I'm honored to have you join me in this work. It's hard work. It's contrarian work. It's unconventional wisdom. Thanks for being part of it.

As you turn the humancentric philosophy and 6 Es framework into action, I'd love to hear from you. I'm inspired regularly by how my fellow humans are implementing these ideas to make work more than just another four-letter word.

Visit www.eryceyl.com/SEEbook and let me know what you're up to.

~ 15 ~

EPILOGUE AND GRATITUDE

This book has had many stops and starts.

When I started writing in 2019, it was shaping up to be a gargantuan tome, containing everything I've ever learned or thought about organizations.

I had a sudden flash of insight in December 2019. Like a proper cliché, I was sitting in an ashram in Ahmedabad, India. I wasn't meditating—just visiting—but something about being there, out of my usual routine, helped me realize that, in order to truly be of help to folks like you, I needed to just write *a* book, not *the* book. I scrapped almost everything I'd written up to that point, scratched out a new outline in a notebook, and started writing on my laptop as my wife and I traversed across Rajasthan.

Then, in April 2020, at the height of the pandemic, my wife and I were in the desert in southern California, picking up her 88-year-old mom to come live safely with us in Colorado, and that very laptop was stolen when our car was broken into. Again, like a proper cliché, I hadn't backed anything up, and everything I'd written was lost.

It took months for me to get back to the book, but throughout 2020, I had the opportunity to deliver multiple keynotes and breakout sessions on this book's contents. Audiences and participants asked insightful questions that further developed my thinking and, in some cases, even changed my mind. Gasp!

It wasn't until November 2020 that I found the time and space to write again. Then, in a seven-day flurry of writing, I drafted the bulk of what you've just read. All those false starts and delays had helped to refine and sharpen my ideas to the point that I could simply sit down and let them pour out.

You could file this under "all things happen for a reason," but I prefer to think of it as, "to every thing there is a season." Throughout those years of trying and failing and starting over and being robbed, I also had the chance to test my ideas in the wild. I gave talks at conferences and to organizations, led workshops, helped companies examine their workplace cultures, and coached leaders. With every opportunity to apply the ideas in this book, I further developed these ideas, refined them, simplified them where that was helpful, and complicated them where *that* was helpful.

In other words, all those delays helped make this book better.

Equally important—and I know I don't have to tell you this— so much changed since this book's inception in 2019. The confluence of a global health crisis, an accelerating climate emergency, and rapid awakening to entrenched social injustices changed—and is still changing—everything, including the world of work.

Through all of this turmoil, many of us re-evaluated our relationship with work. We reassessed the role work plays in our lives. We recalibrated the amount of our lives we were willing to give to our jobs. We reimagined what work could be.

While pundits coined endless new terms—"Great Resignation" and "quiet quitting" among the more annoying—the rest of us realized that work didn't have to be the way it had always been. We could work less without being bad people. We could insist on being treated with dignity, respect, and appreciation. We could ask for more—more autonomy, more flexibility, more pay, more time off, more recognition of our contributions. We could choose to work in circumstances that weren't just about exchanging our time for money, but actually helped us become more satisfied, fulfilled, self-actualized, and flourishing humans.

It wasn't all roses and iced lattes, of course. Many of us lost our jobs. Many of us were treated poorly by our fellow humans. Many of us struggled against systemic racism, sexism, ableism, ageism, homophobia, transphobia, and many other forms of oppression. Some of us lost our lives or had our lives taken from us. Some of us developed chronic health conditions that we're still living with.

And as a job increasingly became "a thing we do" instead of "a place we go," many of us experienced profound isolation, loneliness, and depression. In November 2022, my father died, making it both more difficult to finish this book and more imperative.

And in this landscape of relentless change, I saw hope—hope for a better world and hope for better work. The need for humancentric workplaces became more urgent. This book felt more necessary and more valuable than ever, and I knew I had to share it.

But this book didn't just spring from my head unaided. While our culture loves the great man theory, I'm a very ordinary man, surrounded by an extraordinary community of friends, family, colleagues, and mentors who collaborated —some without even knowing it—to write this book. And I'd like to end by expressing my gratitude to them.

While I don't like to rank people, there's no one more deserving of my gratitude than my wife, Mare Trevathan. She has not only seen every iteration of this book through its ups and downs, she has listened to my half-baked ideas as they've become, well, more-baked. She's read the book out loud to me to help me spot opportunities for clarification or just better writing. As a professional voiceover actor and audiobook narrator, she's mentored me in how to properly record the audio version of this book. She's cheered me on, challenged me, held me to account, supported me, and loved me through this whole process. And if you need someone to give their voice to *your* audiobook, look her up.

My editor Leah Charney's fingerprints are on every page of this book. She didn't just look at this book as a project, but engaged with its ideas and asked me provocative questions —not only about word choice and sentence structure, but about the philosophy and concepts guiding the book. She helped me stay true to my vision and my values, and continually reminded me to keep my *self* in the book. I am forever grateful for her friendship and unfailing support of my work over the years. Track her down if you've got a manuscript that needs a keen and collaborative eye.

The illustrator of this book, Chantel Botha, might not identify as an illustrator at all, but when I first saw her sketch notes, I knew we had to collaborate. Chantel and I got to know each other when she spontaneously created a sketch note version of an article I published early in the pandemic. Since then we've collaborated on many things and become friends, though we've never been on the same continent together, much less in the same room. Though she runs her own company, helping organizations improve life for their customers and employees, Chantel was willing to take on the project of illustrating this book, and her images are absolutely invaluable for conveying my sometimes-abstract concepts through clear, imaginative visuals. If you're looking for training for your organization in customer experience, employee experience, or brand experience, check out Chantel's company, BrandLove.

At the risk of boring you, dear reader, with a list of names, only some of whom you might know, I'll wrap up with just some of the folks who've helped me with encouragement, advice, argument, coffee, beers, love, meals, conversations, and opportunities to develop and test these concepts in the real world: Aleana Reeves, Angela Beloian, Ani Vattano, Beth Gietl, Bob Azman, Bob Heavers, Bob Tipton, Brian Boucher, Chris Doyle, Chris Duncan, Claudette Rowley, Clint Payne, David Dye, David Schoenberg, David Wales, Debbie Shumake, Ed Bodensiek, Eleanor Allen, Eric Hozempa, Eric Spencer, Erin Cox, Fletcher Keister, Gary Grundei, GerRee Anderson, Grace Wangeci, Hilary Blair, James Briggs, Jamie Notter, Jason Lauritsen, Jean-Marie De Lange, Jeff Campbell, Jennifer Montague, Jerry Seufert, Jess DeNicola, Jim Walker, Joe Mazza, Johan Botha, John Common, Josh Bernoff, Josh Bersin, Josh Levine, Joy Herbers, Karen Jaw-Madson, Karen Kralios, Karl Sharicz, Kat Mills, Kate Merson, Kelsey Franklin, Kristen Harris, Kym Wootton, Lee Anderson, Liam Griffith, Lou Carbone, Lou Faust, Luba Abrams, Luke Beckett, Mareli Smit, Mark Hamill, Mark Michelson, Marnie Urbach, Mary Sahlin, Meridith Grundei, Michael Arrington, Michelle Moore, Mike Ganyo, Neal Woodson, Nick Allen, Nick Burn, Nick Glimsdahl, Ozy Aloziem, Pablo Otaola, Patty Soltis, Paul Zak, Penni "PK" Key, Pesha Rudnick, Peter Haid, Peter Neill, Richard Kennedy, Rob Wright, Roger Pugsley, Scott Brown, Scott Webber, Sean Choi, Sergio Angeles, Shane Metcalf, Simon Lawler, Sophia Eyl, Terry Cabeen, Tim Creasey, Tim Kuppler, Tom Paterson,

Treena Colby, Vivek Bhaskaran, Wayne Greenberg, and probably a gazillion others that I'm forgetting. I never stood a chance of creating a truly comprehensive list of everyone who has contributed to this book, but I hope that I've at least conveyed two things: (1) we don't do anything alone, and (2) I'm so grateful for my fellow humans.

BEYOND THE BOOK

Do you mean to tell me that this book hasn't completely quenched your thirst for wit and wisdom to make work more human?

That's great!

Head on over to www.ErycEyl.com/SEEbook for downloadable resources and bonus material.

Interested in bringing Eryc to your event or organization for a keynote or workshop on the concepts in this book? Visit www.ErycEyl.com/schedule to chat with Eryc's team.

REFERENCES AND INFLUENCES

I've been thinking about the ideas in this book for years, reworking, refining, and revising as I'm exposed to new challenges, new concepts, and new contexts. Throughout this process, I've consumed volumes of research on the related topics of customer experience, workplace culture, and employee engagement. I've had conversations and debates with brilliant thinkers, conscientious leaders, and beleaguered workers.

What follows is a probably-incomplete list of the articles, books, organizations, and tools that have influenced my thinking, supported my learning, and taught me new ways of seeing. I owe them all a great debt. This book wouldn't exist without them.

Books

- Amabile, T., & Kramer, S. (2011). *The Progress Principle: Using Small Wins to Ignite Joy, Engagement, and Creativity at Work.* Reed Business Education.
- Arbinger Institute. (2010). *Leadership and Self-Deception: Getting Out of the Box.* Macmillan Publishers.
- Argyris, C. (2006). *Overcoming Organizational Defenses: Facilitating Organizational Learning.* Prentice Hall.
- Bernoff, J. (2016). *Writing Without Bullshit: Boost Your Career by Saying What You Mean.* HarperCollins.
- Blanchard, K. A. S. (1982). *The One Minute Manager.* William Morrow.

- Brown, A. M. (2017). *Emergent Strategy: Shaping Change, Changing Worlds*. Amsterdam University Press.
- Cain, S. (2012). *Quiet: The Power of Introverts in a World That Can't Stop Talking*. Crown.
- Covey, S. R. (2000). *Seven Habits of Highly Effective People*. Amsterdam University Press.
- Covey, S. R., & Merrill, R. R. (2008). The SPEED of Trust: The One Thing That Changes Everything. Amsterdam University Press.
- Deci, E., & Ryan, R. M. (1985). *Intrinsic Motivation and Self-Determination in Human Behavior*. Plenum Press.
- Edmondson, A. C. (2018). *The Fearless Organization: Creating Psychological Safety in the Workplace for Learning, Innovation, and Growth*. Wiley.
- Friedman, S. D. (2008). *Total Leadership: Be a Better Leader, Have a Richer Life*. Harvard Business School Press.
- Gilbert, D. (2006). *Stumbling on Happiness*. Vintage.
- Gopnik, A. (2016). *The Gardener and the Carpenter: What the New Science of Child Development Tells Us About the Relationship Between Parents and Children*. Farrar, Straus and Giroux.
- Goulston, M. (2015). *Just Listen: Discover the Secret to Getting Through to Absolutely Anyone*. AMACOM.
- Graeber, D. (2018). *Bullshit Jobs: A Theory*. Simon & Schuster.
- Grey, C. (2005). *A Very Short, Fairly Interesting and Reasonably Cheap Book about Studying Organizations*. SAGE.
- Heath, C., & Heath, D. (2010). *Switch: How to Change Things When Change Is Hard*. Broadway Books.
- Hiatt, J. (2006). *ADKAR: How to Implement Successful Change in Our Personal Lives and Professional Careers*. Prosci.
- Hiatt, J., & Creasey, T. J. (2003). *Change Management: The People Side of Change*. Prosci Research.
- Horgan, A. (2021). *Lost in Work: Escaping Capitalism*. Amsterdam University Press.
- Jaffe, S. (2021). *Work Won't Love You Back: How Devotion to Our Jobs Keeps Us Exploited, Exhausted, and Alone*. Bold Type Books.
- Jaw-Madson, K. (2018). *Culture Your Culture: Innovating Experiences @Work*. Emerald Publishing Limited.

- Lama, D., Cutler, H. C., Lama, D., & Cutler, H. (2005). *The Art Of Happiness At Work.* Riverhead Books.
- LaMarsh, J. (1995). *Changing the Way We Change: Gaining Control of Major Operational Change.* Addison-Wesley.
- Lencioni, P. M. (2012). *The Advantage: Why Organizational Health Trumps Everything Else In Business.* Wiley.
- Lencioni, P., & Stransky, C. (2006). *The Five Dysfunctions of a Team: A Leadership Fable.* Penguin Random House.
- Levine, J. (2018). *Great Mondays: How to Design a Company Culture Employees Love* (1st ed.). McGraw Hill.
- Loehr, J., Loehr, J., & Schwartz, T. (2005). *The Power of Full Engagement: Managing Energy, Not Time, Is the Key to High Performance and Personal Renewal.* Amsterdam University Press.
- Lyubomirsky, S. (2007). *The How of Happiness: A New Approach to Getting the Life You Want.* Penguin.
- Macgregor, D. (1960). *The Human Side of Enterprise.* MSE publications.
- McChrystal, G. S., Collins, T., Silverman, D., & Fussell, C. (2015). *Team of Teams: New Rules of Engagement for a Complex World.* Van Haren Publishing.
- Nayar, V. (2010). *Employees First, Customers Second: Turning Conventional Management Upside Down.* Harvard Business Press.
- Newport, C. (2021). *A World Without Email: Reimagining Work in an Age of Communication Overload.* Portfolio.
- Notter, J., & Grant, M. (2012). *Humanize: How People-centric Organizations Succeed in a Social World.* Que.
- Pink, D. H. (2011). *Drive: The Surprising Truth About What Motivates Us.* Riverhead Books.
- Press, E. (2021). *Dirty Work: Essential Jobs and the Hidden Toll of Inequality in America.* Farrar, Straus and Giroux.
- Ressler, C., & Thompson, J. (2008). *Why Work Sucks and How to Fix it: No Schedules, No Meetings, No Joke-- the Simple Change that Can Make Your Job Terrific.* Portfolio.
- Rock, D. (2009). *Quiet Leadership: Six Steps to Transforming Performance at Work.* HarperCollins.

- Rock, D. (2020). *Your Brain at Work, Revised and Updated: Strategies for Overcoming Distraction, Regaining Focus, and Working Smarter All Day Long.* HarperCollins.
- Rowley, C. (2019). *Cultural Brilliance: The DNA of Organizational Excellence.* Waterside Productions.
- Schein, E., & Schein, P. (2018). *The Corporate Culture Survival Guide* (3rd ed.). Wiley.
- Seligman, M. E. P. (2012). *Flourish: A Visionary New Understanding of Happiness and Well-being.* Simon & Schuster.
- Senge, P. M. (2006). *The Fifth Discipline: The Art and Practice of the Learning Organization.* Doubleday/Currency.
- Sutton, R. I. (2007). *The No Asshole Rule: Building a Civilized Workplace and Surviving One That Isn't.* Warner Business Books.
- Ton, Z. (2014). *The Good Jobs Strategy: How the Smartest Companies Invest in Employees to Lower Costs and Boost Profits.* New Harvest, Houghton Mifflin Harcourt.
- Vengoechea, X. (2022). *Listen Like You Mean It: Reclaiming the Lost Art of True Connection.* Pan/Macmillan.
- Warzel, C., & Petersen, A. H. (2021). *Out of Office: The Big Problem and Bigger Promise of Working from Home.* Van Haren Publishing.
- Yohn, D. L. (2018). *Fusion: How Integrating Brand and Culture Powers the World's Greatest Companies.* Nicholas Brealey.
- Zak, P. J. (2012). *The Moral Molecule: The Source of Love and Prosperity.* Dutton.

Articles

- Azzarello, P. (2018, April 18). *Why people don't do what you say.* Azzarello Group. https://azzarellogroup.com/web/why-people-dont-do-what-you-say/
- Caulkin, S. (2008, February 9). *The rule is simple: be careful what you measure.* The Guardian. https://www.theguardian.com/business/2008/feb/10/businesscomment1
- Deci, E. L., & Ryan, R. M. (2008). *Self-determination theory: A macro-theory of human motivation, development, and health.* Canadian Psychology/Psychologie canadienne, 49(3), 182-185.

- David Rock: "SCARF: a brain-based model for collaborating with and influencing others"
- Future Market Insights (2022, May). Employee Engagement Market Outlook 2022-2032). Future Market Insights. https://www.futuremarketinsights.com/reports/employee-engagement-market
- Gallup, Inc. (2023, February 20). State of the Global Workplace Report - Gallup. Gallup.com. https://www.gallup.com/workplace/349484/state-of-the-global-workplace-2022-report.aspx
- Kahn, W. A. (1990). PSYCHOLOGICAL CONDITIONS OF PERSONAL ENGAGEMENT AND DISENGAGEMENT AT WORK. *Academy of Management Journal*, 33(4), 692–724. https://doi.org/10.2307/256287
- Maslow, A. H. (1943). A theory of human motivation. *Psychological Review*, 50(4), 370–396. https://doi.org/10.1037/h0054346
- Maslow, A. H. (1969). Theory Z. *Journal of Transpersonal Psychology*, 1(2), 31–47.
- Oncken, W., Jr., & L. Wass, D. (1974). Management time: Who's got the monkey? *Harvard Business Review*, 52(6), 75.
- (2021). *Productivity has risen with remote/hybrid working, but worker trust may pose a larger challenge: PwC survey.* PwC. https://www.pwc.com/gx/en/news-room/press-releases/2021/pwc-future-of-work-survey-2021.html
- Ridgway, V. (1956). Dysfunctional Consequences of Performance Measurements. *Administrative Science Quarterly*, 1(2), 240. https://doi.org/10.2307/2390989
- Williamson, A. M., & Feyer, A. M. (2000). Moderate sleep deprivation produces impairments in cognitive and motor performance equivalent to legally prescribed levels of alcohol intoxication. *Occupational and environmental medicine, 57*(10), 649–655. https://doi.org/10.1136/oem.57.10.649
- Wittbrodt, M. T., & Millard-Stafford, M. (2018). Dehydration Impairs Cognitive Performance: A Meta-analysis. *Medicine and science in sports and exercise, 50*(11), 2360–2368. https://doi.org/10.1249/MSS.0000000000001682

Other

- DISC interaction style assessment
- Human Synergistics (creators of the Organizational Culture Inventory)
- *My Next Guest Needs No Introduction* (D. Letterman, Interviewer). (2018). [Video]. Netflix.
- Prosci (global change management training and consulting firm)
- StrengthsFinder assessment (by Gallup)
- Working Genius assessment (by the Table Group)

ABOUT THE AUTHOR

Eryc Eyl believes in a world in which work isn't just a four-letter word, but part of a path to greater satisfaction, fulfillment, self-actualization, and flourishing. He is a speaker, author, coach, consultant, and educator committed to making work more human.

Eryc helps workplaces align their culture with strategic imperatives, and individuals integrate work with a meaningful, fun, and fulfilling life. His expertise comes from three decades of experience with organizations a wide variety of industries, as well as certifications in workplace culture, change management, and customer experience.

Eryc is also a storyteller, playwright, and DJ who holds a Master's degree in education from the University of Colorado, and a Bachelor's degree in literature and film from Vassar College.

To learn how your organization or event can become more human, visit www.ErycEyl.com for information on Eryc's customized speeches, leadership advising, and consulting.

Photo: Erin Cox
elcphoto.com

ABOUT THE ILLUSTRATOR

As the Innovation Magician and Lead Brand Warrior at Brandlove, a global customer-focused innovation and training consultancy, Chantel Botha thrives on delivering passion and purpose by designing value and connection into every experience involving individuals, customers, employees or corporations. Using her background in business economics, computer sciences, customer experience design, coaching, public speaking, e-commerce and strategy, she brings revolutionary originality and EQ to brands and businesses. In addition to a number of social projects, Chantel lives out her passion for people as a certified Virtual Facilitator, Customer Experience Professional, Laughter Yoga and Lego Serious Play facilitator. Learn more at brandloveglobal.com.